D1131149

Majestic Houses

of Banco Nacional de México

Majestic Houses

of Banco Nacional de México

Clara Bargellini

Gustavo Curiel

Martha Fernández

Ignacio González-Polo

Antonio Rubial García

Mayte Sánchez Lozano

Nelly Sigaut

Fomento Cultural Banamex, A. C.

Editorial Coordination
Cándida Fernández de Calderón
Alberto Sarmiento

Madero 17, Centro
06000 México, D.F.

ISBN: 968-700992-6
DL: M-41897-1999

Contents

Page 2.
Iturbide Palace. Mexico City.

Page 4.
Palace of the Count de San Mateo de Valparaíso. Mexico City.

Palace of the Count de San Mateo de Valparaíso. Mexico City.

Obra y Costeo el Señor Dn Miguel de Berrio y Zaldibar Conde de Sn Mateo de Balparaisso del Consejo de su Magestad en el Real y Supremo de Hazienda y Contador Decano Jubilado del Real

Foreword

The majestic houses from the period of the viceroyalty are some of the most important cultural treasures that have been conserved from that era, providing testimony as to what daily life and the social structure were like as well as the artistic tastes of the inhabitants of what was to become Mexico.

These houses have been acquired by Banco Nacional de México, at various points throughout its 115 years of existence, with a dual purpose: to rescue and conserve them as well as to utilize them for offices. They are manifestations of the desire on the part of Grupo Financiero Banamex-Accival to contribute to the preservation and dissemination of the cultural, historical and artistic values of all Mexicans.

This decision, born of social responsibility and historical conscience and which the Bank has resolutely carried out, is reflected in the formation of a collection of works of art which is significant among the great private collections in Mexico. Together with these works, of no less value are the magnificent buildings which the Bank conserves, adapted to new functions, in diverse cities throughout the country.

The volume that we today have the pleasure of presenting signifies another contribution to a better understanding of, as well as the continued conservation of, these extraordinary examples of Mexico's greatness. As one of the authors included in these texts has so eloquently pointed out, one can neither love nor conserve that which one does not profoundly understand. This sums up the fundamental purpose of this book.

In preparing this work, it was indispensable to delve deeply in order to gain an understanding of the history, iconography, architectural characteristics and decoration of these buildings. Fomento Cultural Banamex commissioned a number of specialists, of recognition and prestige, to carry out meticulous studies that would allow us to more precisely appreciate their characteristics and context.

Pages 8 and 9.
House of the Count del Valle de Súchil. Durango.

Palace of the Count de San Mateo de Valparaíso. Mexico City.

Page 12.
Palace of the Count de San Mateo de Valparaíso. Mexico City.

Owing to the fact that these buildings have witnessed three centuries of life under Spanish rule, it is possible to observe in them the civil architectural art employed in the great houses from the viceroyalty of New Spain as well as the most complete manifestations of the diverse styles which were preferred by citizens of the period.

From the Plateresque style of the house of the Montejo family, which synthesizes some of the most esteemed elements from the sixteenth century in its iconography, to the transition toward the Neoclassical at the end of the eighteenth century and beginning of the nineteenth, which can be appreciated in the house of the Canal family, in San Miguel de Allende, Guanajuato, this journey of three centuries has seen the sobriety of the Baroque style from Michoacán, illustrated by the House of the Diezmo, in Morelia, and the innovations of the Neostilo Baroque in the sumptuous constructions created by architect Francisco Antonio Guerrero y Torres for the Marquis del Jaral de Berrio, which contributed to Mexico City's being dubbed the City of Palaces.

Also outstanding is the, perhaps, lesser known house of the Count del Valle de Súchil, in Durango, a masterpiece of architecture that can compete, in magnificence, with any of the others mentioned in the foregoing. These houses speak to us of a particular lifestyle and the great riches of New Spain which granted what today is Mexico a privileged status among the nations of the world.

The conservation of these buildings, respecting their original characteristics, the artistic integration which is possible within the area of architecture, and the new functionality that has been acquired by these majestic houses in recent decades, as well as their emblematic character for an institution which has as its objective a union of the virtues of experience and innovation, fills us with satisfaction. We present this book toward a better understanding of part of the cultural patrimony which should be source of enormous pride for all Mexicans.

ALFREDO HARP HELÚ
Chairman of the
Board of Directors
Grupo Financiero Banamex-Accival, S.A. de C.V.

ROBERTO HERNÁNDEZ RAMÍREZ
Chairman of the
Board of Directors
Banco Nacional de México, S.A.

The House in New Spain

The House in New Spain

"All are magnificent and made at a great cost, which suits such noble and opulent neighbors." This is how Francisco Cervantes de Salazar described the houses in Mexico City in 1554, houses which at the time pertained to a fortress-like city that had been built by the Spanish at the heart of the Mexica Empire, houses which "anyone could say that they weren't houses, rather fortresses" and which had been so constructed "when there were many enemies since the city could not be defended, surrounding it with towers and ramparts."

Martha Fernández

In effect, the warrior character of the first inhabitants of the city that was built just after the conquest of México-Tenochtitlán conditioned the characteristics of their architecture in such a way that their houses were of the type which, effectively, could be classified as fortresses, topped with battlements and fortified towers. Some of them had moats, such as the house of the conquistador Rodrigo de Castañeda which was situated on San Francisco street (today Madero), across from the convent of San Francisco. Although the structures possessed a roughness in their appearance, they also demonstrated elements of fineness. According to the historian quoted in the foregoing, "the jambs and lintels are not of brick or another despicable material, rather of large stones placed with skill," a reference to stonemasonry, and above the doors were the coats of arms of the owners. Additionally, some of these houses, such as that of Alonso de Villaseca, located on what is today Pino Suárez street, had thick golden rings on their entrance doors as a symbol of the wealth of the owners.

On the inside, the spaces were distributed around a central courtyard ringed by pilasters or columns. The grouping of houses pertaining to Dr. Pedro López, for example, on the corner of what are today Argentina and San Ildefonso (or González Obregón) streets, apart from a façade done in dressed stone, featured a courtyard which was "greatly adorned by the columns, also of stone, which form arcades at the sides." Naturally, these courtyards were always filled with plants and garden areas, such as was the house mentioned by Cervantes de Salazar which he described as "quite pleasant."

The roofs were flat, surely done in wood on the inside and paved in some manner on the top where, additionally, were the necessary "wooden or metal channels through which the rainwater would fall to the street" which were placed along the cornices. Most interesting is that the roofs were not only the tops of the buildings but were, since the beginning, utilized as areas for relaxation and sunbathing, decorated with plants and even tapestries on the days when the owners entertained.

An important characteristic of these houses was their height, which did not exceed two stories, the reason being that "their excess elevation not be the cause of their ruin, with the earthquakes that . . . frequently occur in this land" and, additionally, so that "all receive the sun equally, without one casting a shadow on another" and, finally, "so that the city may be healthier, not having very high buildings that might impede the diverse winds which, with the help of the sun, dissipate and distance the foul miasmas from the neighboring lagoon."

Among all of the houses in Mexico City during this period, outstanding in terms of size and characteristics was the grouping of houses belonging to Hernán Cortés. They were so large that, according to Francisco Cervantes de Salazar, they appeared more like an independent city. They covered the area delimited by what are today Isabel la Católica, Monte de Piedad, Tacuba and Madero streets. These houses included a walkway on the roof which served as an overlook, onto the street, and featured a series of arches supported by columns as well as a railing comprised of stone balusters "so that no one ran the risk of falling." Of course, in addition there were fortified towers, and the walls were topped with battlements.

Once military control over the indigenous population had been consolidated, a change began to occur in the city, brought about by a process of internal transformation within the inhabitants. It was described by Edmundo O'Gorman as one in which "a warrior core of strong internal cohesion begins to suffer a gradual debilitation, with the tendency toward converting it into a group comprised of individuals subject no longer to the rigid and immediate military ties but to the gentler and more distant ties that are created by common interests emerging among them in their positions and activities as citizens. That is to say, the process in which the individual goes from warrior type to citizen type: from conquistador to colonist."

It was thus that the houses which before tended to appear as fortresses began to experience transformations, although not with regard the distribution of the principal interior spaces. They lost their battlements and, in many cases, the fortified towers. The stone walls were plastered, balconies and galleries were opened and the façades were decorated, some with allegorical figures and others with scenes from a particular event. Among the houses from the sixteenth century that still conserve these characteristics is that which pertained to the Montejo family, in Mérida, Yucatán, which today is the property of Banco Nacional de México (BANAMEX) and to which one of the chapters of this book is dedicated, and another which is known as "The House of the One Who Killed the Animal," in the city of Puebla, on whose entrance portal can be admired a hunting scene carved in stone. The interior walls were not only hung with paintings and tapestries but, also, became canvases themselves, such as with the painting *Triunfos*, by Petarca, which is still preserved today in what once was the home of Don Tomás de la Plaza, Dean of the Cathedral of Puebla, the so-called "City of Angels." The foregoing reveals that the houses of New Spain in the sixteenth century, apart from manifestations of the opulence of their owners, reflected the cultural ambiance of the period.

From an artistic point of view, we can say that the changes undergone by the houses in New Spain throughout the sixteenth century pertained to the artistic movement known as Mannerism, although reinterpreted by the artists in the region and not exempt from ornamental elements taken from the Plateresque repertoire. This is important in that, apart from the changes that the society of New Spain was undergoing, as described in the foregoing, there was an interconnected historical process whose roots are to be found in a series of factors that encouraged a boom in the cities during the last third of the sixteenth century. Such factors can be summed up in what has been called "the death of the first plan for the life of New Spain." This original plan consisted of a world, a new world, whose structure was based on rural convents, founded and governed by the religious friars charged with the task of evangelizing the indigenous population. A world whose economic base was founded on the system of workshops and *encomiendas* (the properties and indigenous laborers granted Spanish colonists by royal decree), and whose political structure began to feel increasing removed from the Spanish Crown.

In order to gain greater control over the Indies, the Spanish government effected a series of changes which gave rise to the second, and definitive, plan for the life of New Spain, such as the abolition of the *encomiendas* and the promotion of a system of haciendas which, among other things, included the elimination of the obligation that a hacienda owner live on his estate, as was the case with the *encomiendas*. And as a counterweight to the friars, the presence of a secular clergy was reinforced, whose headquarters were to be found in the cathedrals. Both factors, among others, led to social, political, economic and religious life being developed in the cities rather than in the countryside, significantly increasing the importance of urban centers.

To this can be added other elements – perhaps more important in understanding the artistic personality of New Spain – such as the birth of the "Creole culture." Its most important characteristic was the necessity for these Spaniards who had been born in New Spain to discover their own personality, apart from that of the indigenous peoples and those who were of Spanish birth. In doing so, they undertook a search for cultural elements of universal validity, such as their own classical past which was, in this case, the pre-Columbian cultures, as well as the veneration of their own miraculous religious images, such as the Virgin of Guadalupe and, finally, the exaltation of "Mexican greatness."

The cities, at the center of this panorama, had become de facto centers of civil and religious power, inhabited by the most lofty personages of the nobility born or residing in New Spain. As such, they needed to exhibit an appearance that

Los Triunfos by Petrarca.
House of the Dean. Puebla.

·SIBILLA·ERITTHREA·ÆTATE·20·
·PROPHETAVIT·

corresponded to their importance which was, for them (and, in fact, in reality), comparable to the most important European cities. Puebla had been laid out by angels and Mexico City was "the Venice of the Americas." It was now not enough just to erect functional or merely beautiful buildings as they needed to be in step with the artistic vanguard of the Old World. In the last quarter of the sixteenth century, the residents of New Spain found, in the movement that is known today as Mannerism, the answer that satisfied their artistic needs.

Mannerism is an art that is refined, urbane and secular, based on the rules of known Classical art and codified through architectural treatises. It is also, however, an art that sought new solutions in that although the rules were precise, they were altered and reinterpreted. In Europe, apart from the treatises, many artists had the opportunity to visit the works from the classical world as well as those by whom we now classify as Mannerist architects. This was not the case of artists in New Spain, whose education at the time was fundamentally liberal. In New Spain as well as in Europe, however, both the treatises and the works were simply points of departure in the carrying out of interpretations, recreations and, finally, original creations with their own, regional characteristics.

In New Spain, Mannerism experienced two periods of creation. The first began in the year 1559 when the architect Claudio de Arciniega built the Imperial Catafalque in memory of Charles V, in the Chapel of San José de los Naturales, within the convent of San Francisco, in Mexico City. This first stage, which lasted until the 1630s, is characterized by an apparent experimentation in that it was a period in which the artistic elements that were to define the architectural traditions of New Spain had not yet been determined. It was a stage in which solutions from diverse architectural traditions, such as the Gothic and the Mudejar, were combined, or new solutions were invented in order to resolve concrete problems, such as the orthogonal ribs. The buildings most representative of this period were, without a doubt, the new and definitive cathedrals that had begun to be constructed precisely at the midpoint of the sixteenth century, when the cities were acquiring the importance that they still preserve today. These cathedrals did not then conform to a unified program that extended throughout New Spain and, as such, each was designed in a unique manner. For example, those in Mérida and Guadalajara had only three naves while the one in Mexico City was originally designed with seven. In the end, it and the Cathedral of Puebla were constructed with five naves. No cupola was originally planned for the Cathedral of Mexico City while that in Mérida boasts the oldest dome in New Spain, completed by the architect Juan Miguel de Agüero in 1598.

From this, we can understand that the houses that were constructed or remodeled in New Spain during the second half of the sixteenth century did not follow a defined program, at least in terms of their decorative elements. Hence, the combination of Mannerism and Plateresque in palaces such as that of the Montejo family, or of Mannerism and the indigenous interpretation of European models, known as *tequitqui*, in "The House of the One Who Killed the Animal."

The House of the One Who Killed the Animal. Puebla.

Although there is a lack of research on the subject, the affirmation has been accepted as valid that it was in the seventeenth century when the types of residential structures multiplied in New Spain to such a degree that, from this period onward, there appeared a mixture of majestic houses, detached houses and a type of multi-unit building known as a *vecindad*. Unfortunately, very few houses from the period have conserved their original characteristics since the majority were transformed in later eras. We can, however, turn to a number of literary and graphic accounts to get an idea of their possible characteristics. For example, Friar Juan de Torquemada affirmed that the houses of Mexico City were of stonemasonry, "large and tall, with many large windows, balconies and iron railings of fine workmanship." This implies that they were houses filled with light thanks to their many large, rectangular windows and the balconies with opened onto the streets. Although he doesn't state precisely how large or tall the houses were, the dimensions couldn't have been exceedingly great as the inhabitants of the capital lived in constant fear of earthquakes and the fragility of the subsoil.

Tomás Gage was aware of this when he wrote, in 1625, that "the buildings are of stone and good bricks: but they are not tall, because of the frequent earthquakes suffered in this clime, and which could be demolished if they had more than three floors." The rooms continued to be distributed around a courtyard that served as a garden area "to provide recreation and comfort for those who lived there."

Graphic testimony of what Mexico City looked like at the beginning of the seventeenth century can be found in the drawing titled *Forma y levantado de la ciudad de México* (Shape and Survey of Mexico City) which was created by Juan Gómez de Trasmonte, in 1628. This perspective drawing depicts the city as viewed, approximately, from the area of Chapultepec Park and gives the impression that the houses had double-pitched roofs with glazed ceramic tiles which, of course, was quite removed from reality. Therefore, more than a portrait, it seems a catalog of conventions that did, however, gave rise to the legend that claims that the houses of the seventeenth century failed to reflect the richness of the religious architecture. This is difficult to believe when compared to what we have observed with respect to the characteristics of the civil architecture from the preceding century.

It is worth examining the development of architecture in New Spain during the seventeenth century in order to perhaps find another explanation which might justify this legend. Between the 1630s and the 1680s, we can observe the parallel evolution of two artistic movements: the second period of creation in Mannerism and what might be called "the mid-century eclecticism." The second period of Mannerism in New Spain was characterized, fundamentally, by the establishment of various elements that could be qualified as constants in the architecture of New Spain such as, for example, the entrances featuring superimposed religious images which gave rise to the term "portal-altarpiece," cathedrals with five naves, and churches with barrel-vaulted roofs with lunettes and cupolas at the transepts.

The movement which has been categorized as eclectic coincided, temporarily, with this second period of Mannerism and demonstrated a combination of elements of various artistic styles and modalities while at the same time introducing

The Principal Plaza of Mexico City. Folding screen. 17th century. Collection of Rodrigo Rivero Lake.

Pages 24 and 25.
Forma y levantado de la ciudad de México, by Juan Gómez de Trasmonte. Collection of the Museo de la Ciudad de México.

Forma y Levantado

Por la correspondencia de los numeros se s

Nº 1. Conuentos de S. Fran.co	4.	q. son S.t Fran.co S. Tiago S. Diego S.ta Maria la redonda.	Nº
Nº 2. de S.t Augustin	4.	S.t Augustin S. Pablo. S. Seuastiaen, S. Cruz	
Nº 3. de S. Domingo.	2.	que son S. Domingo y Porta Cœli.	Nº
Nº 4. Padres de la Comp.a	4.	Casa professa los estudios, S. Ilefonso S. Anna nouciada	
Nº 5. Mercenarios	2.	Nuestra S.a de la merced y Nu S.ra de Belem.	Nº
Nº 6. Nra S.ra del Carmen	y	N.ra Sennora do Montserrato	Nº

Suma 18:

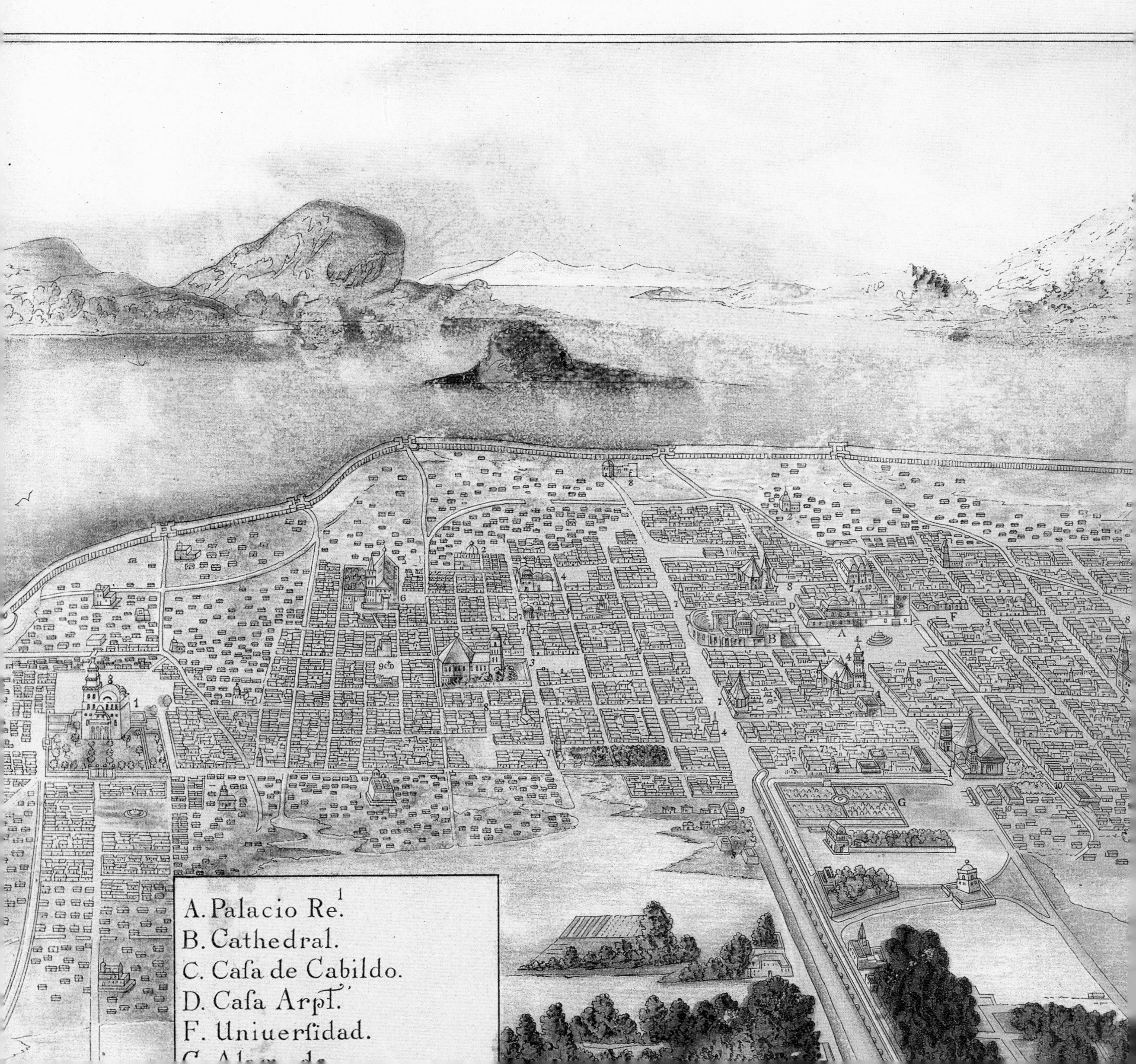

LA CIVDAD DE MEXICO.

n En Esta Copia los conuentos y cosas señalados.

xas. Sa Catharina de Sena La Encarnacion Sa Ynes Sa Teresa, Jhs Maria La conception San Laurenço, Las descalças Sa Clara S. Juo de La pœnitencia Regina cœli Sa Monica las recoxidas y S. Gero Suma 14

itales Hospital Rl de los Yndios de Nra Sra de Lamor de Dios del Spiritu S. de Juan de Dioz de La miseri, cordia de St Hijpolito y de San Laçaro

oquias. 2 Sta Catharina Martijr, y La Vera Cruz

gios El de Sanctos S. Juan de Latran Colegio de Xpo, Colegio de Las niñas.

Suma 4:

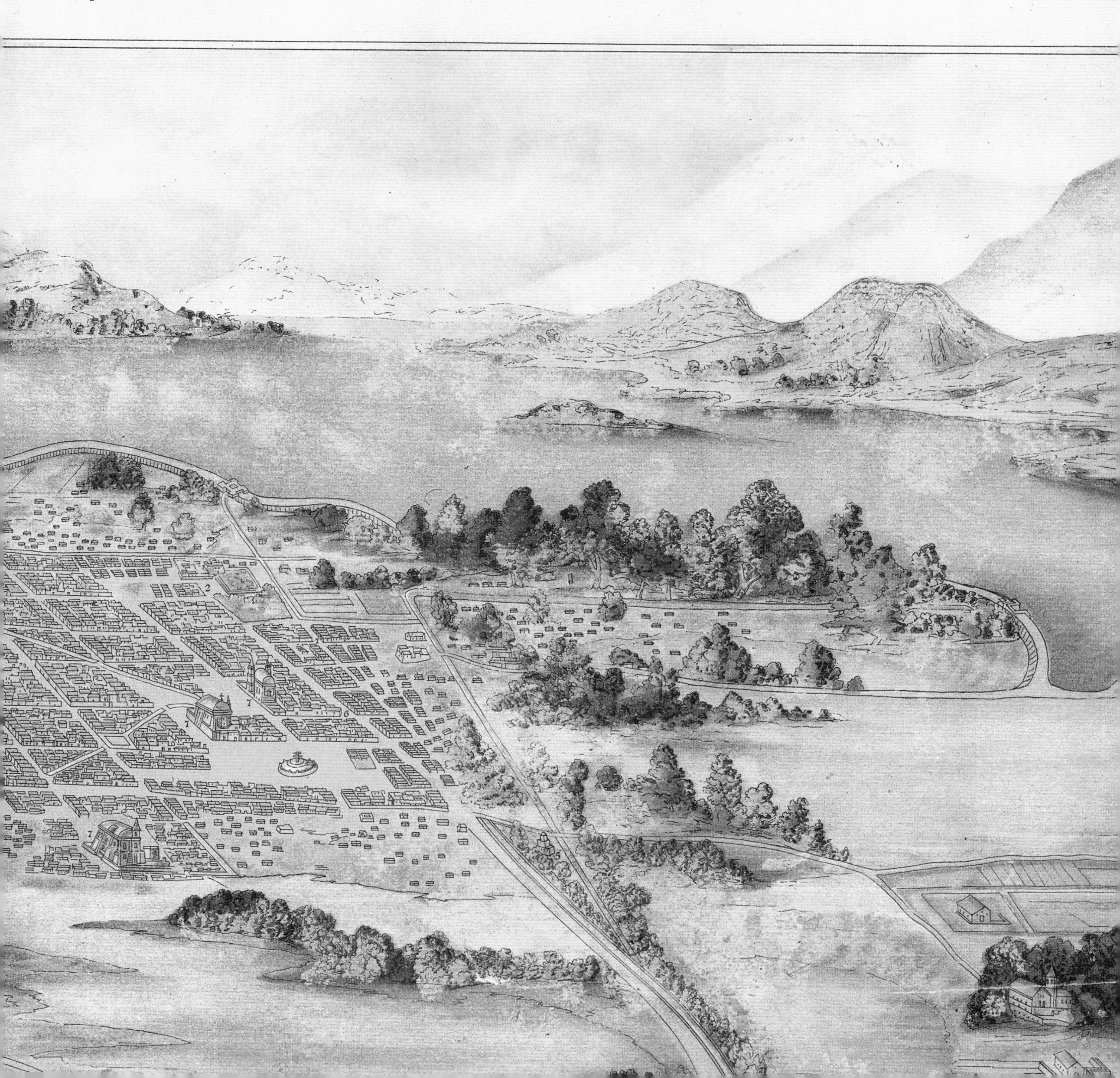

important novelties, indicating that Mannerism, as a unified style, was beginning to go out of fashion and that a change was occurring which was to produce the style that we know as Baroque. The four areas in which the architects from the period demonstrated innovation in their production were the abundance of ornamentation, a marked tendency toward chiaroscuro effects, the design of portals with ascending lines and ornamentation of mixed styles of lines. All of the foregoing was enriched with elements from the Gothic style, for example the ubiquitous employment of the small pyramid-shaped indentations utilized to highlight the spandrels of arches. Although there are many works that we could cite which exemplify this style, three of the most important are found in Mexico City: the churches which pertained to the convent of La Concepción, those pertaining to the convent of San José de Gracia, and the church which was the Oratorio de San Felipe Neri, el Viejo, of which only the portal remains today.

Perhaps the two most important elements introduced at the time, however, were the twin entrances to the churches pertaining to the convents, including the three just mentioned, which constituted a spatial novelty unique to New Spain, and the adoption of the Solomonic column in the Altar of the Kings in the Cathedral of Puebla, a work executed by Lucas Méndez between 1646 and 1650. The latter element was so successfully adopted by the architecture of New Spain that we can speak of a distinct, new Baroque architecture which was created in this country, beginning with the incorporation of the first Solomonic columns in the Cathedral of Mexico City by the architect Cristóbal de Medina, between 1684 and 1689. As such, it can be stated that what has been categorized as Solomonic Baroque constituted the first modality of Mexican Baroque and was doubtless one of the most important.

The Baroque style, a manifestation characterized as having led to the alteration of the rules of Classical art, for being an art fundamentally sensual and very theatrical, was the art par exellence of the Creole society in that the process of searching for the personality of New Spain reached its denouement at this point, precisely when the search was ended and an identity established. Although it is often supposed that this occurred during the Enlightenment, as the precursor to the nationalistic sentiments that emerged with the Independence movement, in reality it can be said – and has been by Edmundo O'Gorman – that the complete Creole maturity was achieved in the seventeenth century. It was in that century that we can see cities like Puebla and Mexico City begin to acquire the physiognomy that we know today, the century of Don Carlos de Sigüenza y Góngora and of Sor Juana Inés de la Cruz.

Although the Solomonic support was utilized greatly in religious architecture, it appears not to have been employed in the civil architecture within New Spain, at least during the seventeenth century. This was perhaps due to the symbolic significance these types of supports possessed. According to Christian tradition, the Temple of Solomon was designed by God and included helicoid columns in the entrance portico. As such, these columns marked the entrance into the house of the Divinity, perhaps inspiring a reluctance to employ them in civil architecture or, in other words, in spaces utilized or lived in by mortals.

The fact that houses failed to employ Solomonic columns did not, however, mean that they were devoid of any type of ornamentation. As noted previously, although few houses from the period remain, worthy of note is one to be found in the city of Puebla which demonstrates that the inhabitants of New Spain reflected, in their own homes, the artistic changes to be found in the churches. The house in question is the well-known Casa de las Bóvedas (House of the Vaults), constructed between 1684 and 1685 by the architect Diego de la Sierra and destined for occupation by the prebendary of the city's cathedral, Don Diego Peláez Sánchez. Its name is derived from the fact that the entire house was executed with vaulted ceilings, on both of its floors, a fact that caused great amazement at the time, moving one person to state that "there hasn't been anyone who hasn't praised them."

The house is truly interesting. As was mentioned, it is of two stories and has a north-south orientation. The façade suffered modifications in the eighteenth century during which the jambs of the square windows were extended to the height of the cornice and ornamentation of bricks and glazed ceramic tiles was added. The entrance is found to the extreme east side of the house, is of right angles and bears no more ornamentation than a relief allusive to the life of St. Francis.

Of what we can consider to be the work of Diego de la Sierra on the façade, outstanding is the upper volume in which the following elements are of great relevance: the bossed pilasters, the "tritostyle" half-columns that are placed against them, the double pediment that tops the windows and the asymmetry of the fenestration. All of the foregoing elements serve to demonstrate two of the factors employed in religious architecture since the middle of the seventeenth century: the taste for chiaroscuro and ornamental richness.

With regard to the double pediment above the windows, it should be noted that there exists a precedent in the portal of the Church of Jesús de Roma, a work from about 1600 by Giácomo de la Porta. This solution was repeated, with slight variations, by Diego de la Sierra in the entrance and courtyard of the house in Puebla.

On the inside, the rooms are to be found – as with all the houses from the period – distributed around a courtyard, the central courtyard, but it is here where the elements of interest become multiplied, especially with regard to the vaults, the buttress pillars, the isolated supports and the arches. The vaults that cover the house are varied in that each space features a different type of solution. Some are groined, others have arrises and yet others are ornamented with geometric figures, while the cupola above the staircase is finished with echinus molding. There are similar variations among the arches: some are angular while others are curved, and those on the upper level feature vigorous striation. It is impossible to determine where the architect found his inspiration for these surprising solutions, but the work as a whole is allusive to the Arabic features of palaces such as Alhambra, near Granada, and Alcázar, in Seville.

The buttress pillars respond to the same principle as the classics, a square pillar to which are affixed half-columns, although in this house the half-columns, rather than centered on the buttress pillars so as to leave exposed the corners of same, were designed by the architect to extend to the corners of each face of the pillars, producing the effect not of attachment but, rather, of curling around the pillars, a solution that pertains to the Plateresque repertoire as can be observed, for example, in the support elements of the courtyards of the former Hospital de los Reyes Católicos in the city of Santiago de Compostela.

The isolated supports of the courtyard are also varied: some are unadorned columns of the Doric order while others are "tritostyle," like those of the façade, and still others are pillars to which only a single half-column is attached. The pillars on the second floor feature an undulating striation that continues upward and into the arches themselves, producing a sense of vibration in the courtyard which recalls the proposals by the Italian architect Guarino Guarini, as expressed in his treatise entitled *Disegni d'architettura civile et eclesiástica*, published in 1686, but which quite probably was a mere codification of solutions that had already been executed in Europe at the time.

In the end, we have timeworn solutions combined with others which are avant-garde. With further regard to the Casa de las Bovedas, it is important to note that although there are no Solomonic columns, the use of striation with movement (undulating and zigzagging) is to be found within the elements pertaining to the Orden Salomónico Entero (Complete Solomonic Order) conceived by Friar Juan de Ricci which was equivalent, with certain variations, to the Supreme Corinthian Order proposed by Guarino Guarini. At any rate, it remains a house completely Baroque. Likewise, it is also worthy of note that, in more than one sense, the solutions employed in the courtyard of the house of the Count del Valle de Súchil, in Durango, to which one of the studies in this book is dedicated, remind us of the house constructed by Diego de la Sierra.

Just as in Puebla, similar manifestations were occurring in the rest of the cities in New Spain. Mexico City, of course, was no exception, proof of which is the depiction of the Viceroy's Palace offered by the painter Cristóbal de Villalpando in his work featuring Mexico City's principal plaza. In it, the arches and pillars of the central courtyard are to be found completely bossed while the entrance portal presents rich ornamentation. With regard to the houses in general from the period, the graphic testimony that exists is not as eloquent in this sense, such as the case of the panorama of the city found on the reverse side of the folding screen *Biombo de la Conquista*, conserved in the Museo Franz Meyer, and another attributed to the painter Diego Correa, also in the form of a folding screen, which had belonged to the Count de Moctezuma and is conserved in the Museo Nacional de Historia within Chapultepec Castle.

In both works, the houses are of one or two stories, with flat roofs and courtyards. It is noteworthy that vaults can be seen on the roofs of a number of these houses, certainly related to the special requirements in topping staircases and private chapels contained in these homes. Their façades, on the other hand, are quite plain, highlighted here and there by railings of forged iron which covered balconies and windows. These characteristics were confirmed by Friar

Casa de las Bovedas. Puebla.

Pages 30 and 31.
Panorama of Mexico City. Folding screen.
Collection of the Museo Franz Meyer.

BUAP

Agustín de Vetancurt, in his *Teatro mexicano*, in which he states that the buildings in Mexico City "had upper and lower floors with attractive balconies, and large windows with iron grating elaborated with great skill . . . ." It is important to reiterate that, in this period, the houses were of, at most, two stories.

As in any city, not all of the houses in Mexico City were grand palaces. There were also less sumptuous houses, as evidenced by the folding screens just mentioned as well as a great quantity of documents from the period. One of them, for instance, describes a house in Mexico City, in 1696, as being "small, tall with a storefront . . . comprised of a storefront, entrance door, vestibule, courtyard and in it a room and stables, its staircase that rises to [an upper corridor along which is a] living room, bedroom and another room with its walls of masonry of *tezontle* stone, the ceilings of beams . . . and the roofs paved with bricks . . . ." From this account, we can infer that these houses had given over their lower levels to commercial storefronts while on the upper levels were to be found the living quarters of the owners, all of which were distributed around a single courtyard.

Among the complex of houses depicted on the aforementioned folding screens, also discernible are the *vecindades*. Although we know little about this type of housing in the seventeenth century, it appears that, as with the other houses, they were of one or two floors whose rooms were distributed around a courtyard. Another document from the end of the century talks of a building that had been proposed by architect Cristóbal de Medina and seems to refer precisely to a *vecindad*. It was to have two levels with a staircase leading to the central courtyard, and each of the units was to have two rooms. Presumably, the service areas of the building, such as toilets, kitchen, stables, etc., would be communal and would have to be shared by all of the *vecinos*, or neighbors.

Although the graphic testimony does not allow us to see, nor do the historical documents specify, it is important to note that all of the houses (even the grand palaces) in New Spain included storefronts on the lower levels where there were shops or artisans' workshops. This formed part of the life of the cities and the rent received provided an income for the owners. The storefronts opened onto the streets only and were not connected directly to the interior areas of the house. They tended to have a public area and a small back room, or they featured a makeshift mezzanine which served as living quarters for the shop owners and artisans or as storage space for their implements or merchandise. This latter type of storefront was known as a "cup and saucer."

The eighteenth century, that of the Enlightenment, was of capital importance to the development of Baroque architecture in New Spain. While the so-called Solomonic Baroque continued to experience growth and enrichment, new modalities were created. As a whole, they achieved a consolidation in the most significant and representative Baroque architecture from the period of the viceroyalty, as well as the most spectacular. Among these new modalities, three were especially significant: the Estípite Baroque, the Anastilo Baroque and the Neostilo Baroque. The first was specifically characterized by the use of the *estípite* pilaster, that which is in the shape of an inverted pyramid with a truncated base, and can be appreciated in works such as the entrance to the Sagrario Metropolitano and in the churches of both San Francisco Javier, in Tepotzotlán, and San Felipe Neri, el Nuevo, in Mexico City, to cite just three examples. The Anastilo Baroque was so named because it exhibited a lack of tectonic supports such as columns or pilasters, in such a way that the works are formed by ornamental and symbolic elements and, in the majority of cases, by pilaster-base elements. This modality can be observed, for example, in the entrance to the Church of San Diego de Guanajuato.

The Neostilo Baroque, in the simplest of terms, can be defined as a return to the column and the pilaster (with the exception of the *estípite*) yet with something more. On one hand, the Neostilo became a sort of summary of all of the architecture in New Spain, from Mannerism to Anastilo while, on the other hand, it was a reinterpretation of all of the elements and styles employed by the architects up until this point, at the same time forming a code of new architectural proposals. In other words, it turned out to be a sort of encyclopedia or treatise on built architecture as well as a search for solutions more in accordance with modern times, both characteristics closely related to the mind set of the Enlightenment. It can be affirmed that the Neostilo became the final modality of the Baroque in New Spain and the first of the Enlightenment, as experienced in the viceroyalty. Examples of Neostilo are the entrance to the Church of La Enseñanza, in Mexico City, the Oratorio de San Felipe Neri, in the city of Querétaro, the Parish Church of Santa Prisca, in Taxco, the entrance to the Santa Casa de Loreto, in San Miguel de Allende, and the Parish Church of Santiago Tianguistengo, in the state of México, to mention just a few of the many works. It is interesting to note that the last three of the aforementioned incorporate Solomonic columns but not of the type employed in New Spain in the previous century, of a twisted design and whose model is similar to the design included by architect Giacomo Barozzi da Vignola in his treatise entitled *Regola delli Cinque Ordini d'Architettura*. Rather, these were columns of an undulating design, closer to those employed in Italy, taking as their model the Colonna Santa and the Baldacchino de San Pedro.

With respect to the houses, José Antonio de Villaseñor y Sánchez wrote, between 1746 and 1748, that those in Mexico City "have been elaborated with greater meticulousness and, thus, although the number of its inhabitants has grown, they have been accommodated in less formal space, by occupying the air with their height, enclosing in a lesser perimeter the great magnificence of the city." This seems to mark the point when a mezzanine began to be added to the traditional two-level construction, the extra level becoming a characteristic of the eighteenth-century palaces of New Spain. Their presence was surely due to the more complex needs of the society during this period. The ground floor continued to house storefronts and the upper floor was still the principal space while the mezzanine could be used for offices in which the owners could oversee their businesses or as warehouses for storing products brought to the city from their haciendas. Additionally, the space often included living quarters for the male servants of the houses.

Naturally, the presence of a mezzanine modified, to a certain extent, the spatial sense of the houses. The mezzanine level opened onto the courtyard only by means of windows and, as such, the arcades surrounding the courtyard rose to the wooden ceiling which formed the floor of the upper level. With this solution, the lower supports were of greater height than those of the second floor, and the visual impression created was that of greater size and openness in the courtyard.

Certainly, not all of the courtyards of the houses throughout New Spain were the same as those to be found in Mexico City. Proof of this can be seen in the courtyards of the Baroque houses that have been conserved in the city of Querétaro. These are delimited by pillars or columns with Tuscan capitals, of one story in height and which support arches, occasionally decorated with figures elaborated in stucco. It is the arches which are the elements most characteristic of these courtyards in that they offer the most variety of form: mixtilinear, lobed or quarter-round, accompanied by large, bead moldings that are also of diverse forms, and included the ogee arch of Gothic origin. As examples, we can cite the house of the Marquis del Villar del Águila, that of Captain Don José de Escandón, Count de Sierra Gorda, that of the Marquis de Rayas, today the headquarters of the Secretaría de Cultura y Bienestar Social (Ministry of Culture and Social Well-being) and, of course, the house of the Marquise del Villar del Águila, Gertrudis Josefa de Villanueva Freire.

Another fundamental element of civil architecture are the niches that were created on the upper corners of many of the houses. Certainly, their presence was due to the religious sentiments held by the residents of the period, but their true function within the urban design of the city is not fully understood. It is possible to deduce, however, that they perhaps served to guide the religious processions that moved through the streets during festivities such as those of Holy Week.

From an artistic aspect, within that which is generically known as Solomonic Baroque, three classes of supports were employed during the eighteenth century. First were the helicoid columns similar to those used in the previous century (an example of which can be found at the entrance to the convent of Santa Mónica de Guadalajara) such as can be admired in the staircase of the former Customs building in the city of Puebla. The second type were the aforementioned Neostilo which do not seem to have been used in the civil architecture of New Spain, and the third was the Solomonic pilaster, with the undulating ornamentation, proposed by Guarino Guarini in the treatise cited earlier. This type can be appreciated in the entrance to the Church of San Juan de Dios, in Mexico City, constructed by architect Miguel Custodio Durán, and is accompanied by other interesting elements such as the cornices and the undulating lines at the top. Cornices of this nature were employed in religious architecture and can also be observed in one of the cupolas of the ruined Church of San Lázaro, in Mexico City, again the work of Custodio Durán, but the most interesting is that they were also employed, with a certain profusion, in civil architecture, especially in the cities of Puebla and Durango.

House of the Marquise del Villar del Águila. Querétaro.

Although the *estípite* was not common to civil architecture, there are important

examples to be found in Mexico City such as the Palacio de los Mascarones, located on what today is Ribera de San Cosme avenue. This house was the summer estate of the Count del Valle de Orizaba. The first stage of its construction lasted from 1766 until 1771, but the interior remained unfinished until the nineteenth century, when the construction was completed. The façade of the house features strong and majestic *estípite* pilasters which, as in Classical art, serve to support young atlantes, or caryatids, which the public generally refers to as grotesques. The entrance door, also flanked by *estípite* pilasters, features a mixtilinear arch whose keystone has the characteristics of a valance. The windows are supported by bases composed of richly decorated double valances and are finished off with ornamentation which combines moldings that form geometric shapes with naturalistic decoration. The surrounding surfaces are entirely bossed.

Due to its beauty and its originality, the façade of this house has been the object of abundant praise. Manuel Rivera Cambas, for example, commented in 1882 that it was "one of the adornments not only of the San Cosme neighborhood but, also, of the capital."

Within the house are two courtyards. The principal courtyard is surrounded on all four sides by colonnades. The doorway leading into the secondary courtyard is framed by *estípite* pilasters while the windows feature bossed frames whose jambs rise to the height of the cornice. The roof was flat and the ceiling was surely done in wood while the roof's surface was paved. From a spatial point of view, the house presents an important novelty in that it incorporates a basement which, apart from being a habitable space, provided an excellent solution in that it isolated the principal level from the damp and saltpetrous soil.

Like the rest of the houses from the period, the courtyard was filled with plants and served as a virtual garden area while, like a proper country retreat, there was also a quite large garden area to the east which, according to a lithograph from the nineteenth century, featured a series of walkways which radiated outward from a central fountain.

Although lacking *estípite* pilasters as structural elements in their entrances, there are other important houses from the middle of the eighteenth century, in Mexico City, that are worthy of mention here. One is that which served as the principal residence of the aforementioned Count del Valle de Orizaba, known as the Casa de los Azulejos (House of Tiles) and located on the corner of what are today Madero street and Condesa lane. Originally, only the south and west façades had been dressed with glazed ceramic tiles but, at the beginning of the twentieth century, the north façade, which faces what is today Cinco de Mayo avenue, was redone in the same fashion by architect Guillermo Heredia. Legend has it that the Count had a son named Luis de Vivero Ircio de Mendoza who was more inclined to diversion than to work to such a degree that, as a reprimand, he was told: "You will never build a house of tiles" and, afterward, determined that this prophecy not be fulfilled, he went on to carry out the work. The more credible version, as told by Manuel Romero de Terreros, is that Doña Graciana Suárez de Peredo, the fifth Countess del Valle de Orizaba, originally from the city

House of the Count del Valle de Súchil. Durango.

of Puebla, brought with her to Mexico City the fashion of finishing façades with tiles.

Effectively, one of the principal characteristics of the architecture in Puebla, both civil and religious, was the treatment of walls with brick, glazed ceramic tiles and a stucco-like mortar, creating diverse designs through the combination of these materials, predominantly checkered and crosshatched patterns. A magnificent example of such houses in Puebla that incorporate these materials is one known as the Casa del Alfeñique, commissioned in 1790 by the master ironworker Juan Ignacio Morales and built by the architect Inchaurregui. One of the notable features is the utilization of *estípite* pilasters, of mortar, on the façade.

The aforementioned Casa de los Azulejos, however, presents various differences compared to the houses in Puebla in that it incorporated neither bricks nor mortar but, rather, the material characteristic of construction in Mexico City which was the gray, *chiluca* quarry stone and which resulted in color combinations that were, perhaps, of lesser contrast.

Likewise, from the spatial point of view, the Casa de los Azulejos follows the structural model of the mansions of Mexico City in that it is comprised of two stories plus a mezzanine. The façade contains two niches, one over the principal entrance and another at the top of the corner, and features a mixtilinear cornice. The entrance was executed with right angles and is richly ornamented, framed by pilasters just as is the rest of the façade.

The principal courtyard features columns which are octagonal, "tritostyle" and ornamented, and which support the wooden ceiling. The staircase is of stone and its wainscot and risers are also dressed with glazed ceramic tiles. On the wall of the landing is a mural, by José Clemente Orozco, entitled *Omniciencia*. On one wall of the courtyard is a beautiful, scalloped fountain beneath an arch in the shape of a half star, with three powerful *estípite* pilasters at the rear. Also of note is the entrance to what had been the private chapel which features an arch similar to that above the fountain and an abundance of ornamentation on the pilasters, spandrels and cornice.

From more or less the same period, although today in lamentable condition, is the forgotten palace of the Count of San Bartolomé de Xala, located on what is today Venustiano Carranza street. The arch on the south side of the courtyard bears the inscription: "This house was started on January 1, 1763, and finished on July 31, 1764, Sr. Don Antonio Rodríguez de Soria made it and the master was Don Lorenzo Rodríguez." On the keystone of the same arch is another inscription which reads: "The arch was finished on September 23, 1763." Lorenzo Rodríguez was one of the most important architects in New Spain, and outstanding among his works, for its beauty and importance, is the Sagrario Metropolitano, in Mexico City.

The house is comprised of two levels and a mezzanine. The façade presents a curious asymmetrical solution in that it gives the impression of being what today we would call a duplex. What was originally the principal entrance, to the east, as well as the openings on the mezzanine and upper floor are framed by paneled pilasters of double height whose capitals feature valances of three

Casa de los Azulejos. Mexico City.

points. On the west side, however, the ground-floor level and the mezzanine are separated by a cornice, resulting in pilasters that are only one story in height. They are also paneled but do not include valances. The fenestration at the mezzanine level is also varied, the windows on the east side framed by ornamentation featuring a vegetal motif while those on the east are framed by strong, paneled jambs which rise to the cornice.

In reality, the element that unifies the structure is the second floor. Its balconies are identical, the jambs ornamented with square bosses and undulating moldings while the lintels are decorated with the same bosses and geometric moldings. Unfortunately, one of the windows has, today, completely lost its ornamentation. The entablature is straight and unbroken: the architrave features an undulating molding that seems to be draped over it, the frieze is filled with small rectangular bosses and the cornice is straight, interrupted here and there by the openings for the waterspouts. The inverted arches at the top are evidently from a later intervention.

What was to become the principal volume, where the former door and vestibule were located, lies to the west, and from an artistic point of view is less magnificent. The only outstanding element of the rest of the house is the blind wall on the upper floor on which is found a cross, elaborated in a very dark *tezontle* stone, that served to mark the separation of the two sides of the house, the east and west. Originally, the cross was accompanied by a relief with the monogram of the Virgin Mary while over the entrance was a modillion with the coat of arms of the Count and other ornamentation featuring valances.

As a whole, this entrance possesses one of the elements most characteristic of Baroque architecture in Mexico City: the combination of exposed *tezontle* stone with *chiluca* quarry stone, producing the classic contrast of the colors red and gray in the civil architecture of the capital. *Tezontle* was greatly employed in architecture from the beginning of the period of the viceroyalty. Its lightness aided in reducing the overall weight of the buildings in a city founded on very muddy subsoil and located in a seismic zone. It appears that it wasn't until the eighteenth century, however, that it was left exposed. This novelty was noted by Friar Juan de Viera who wrote, between 1777 and 1778, that the material utilized in the houses was "a stone in the manner of a honeycomb or sponge, rust-colored, so porous and light, that weighs little more than pumice stone and makes such joints with the mortar that the walls become of one piece."

The principal courtyard of the house is square and the roofing over the upper and lower arcades is of wooden beams. On the north and south sides, the roofing over the lower level is supported by depressed arches while on the east and west sides striated columns with beautifully carved wooden capitals are employed. On the upper level, however, the roofing of the entire arcade is supported by columns.

The principal staircase, located in the southeast corner of the courtyard, leads to both the mezzanine and the upper floor. It is of stone and most outstanding are the wainscot and risers covered by glazed ceramic tiles and the candle holder at the landing which is a polychromatic plaster sculpture which depicts a mulatto man dressed in the fashion of the times.

Palacio de los Mascarones.
Mexico City.

In this house from the middle of the eighteenth century, we can observe the insertion of elements that can be considered *neostilo*, such as the pilasters of the façade and the undulating moldings that frame the balconies of the second floor. Among the houses considered most characteristic of this modality of Baroque, however, are those which are dealt with in this book, including the house of the Count of San Mateo de Valparaiso and that of the second Marquis del Jaral de Berrio, today known as the Iturbide Palace, both of which pertain to Banco Nacional de México, as well as that of the Count de Santiago de Calimaya, all the work of architect Francisco Antonio de Guerrero y Torres. One can make a comparison between the texts dedicated to each of these houses in that they all correspond to the general style of the majestic houses of Mexico City, as has been discussed in the foregoing. It is, perhaps, worth noting a number of the characteristics which lead us to include them within the modality of Baroque previously discussed: the utilization of pilasters on the façades, the presence of profuse ornamentation based on vegetal motifs and the employment of moldings in the form of geometric figures, undulating ornamentation and valances.

Perhaps the most interesting things about these houses, however, are the existence of the imposing towers which top their corners and the presence of pre-Columbian elements combined with motifs taken from the classical Greco-Roman repertoire. Although the towers no longer had any sort of defensive function, serving instead as sort of overlooks integrated into the recreational area of what the roofs had become, they continue to remind us of the forbidding towers of the fortified houses of the sixteenth century, causing us to consider that perhaps they form part of the encyclopedic summary of the civil architecture that represented the *neostilo* in New Spain.

The study of pre-Columbian cultures was encouraged and even promoted by Charles III. The interest of the Spanish monarch in the cultures of the past also included the excavation of the cities of Pompeii and Herculaneum which began in 1746 while he also ruled Naples and Sicily. Within the reformist policies that he implemented upon assuming the Spanish throne was the recovery of the historical patrimony of his entire kingdom including, of course, his provinces in the Americas. Convinced that a consciousness of the antiquity of a culture granted it a greatness, during his reign he spelled out the first standards regarding the protection of the artistic patrimony of Spain.

It is not surprising, then, that the study of pre-Columbian cultures was also encouraged in New Spain, resulting in a revaluation of their historical and artistic manifestations. To these general conditions can be added others, more particular, that favored the incorporation of diverse manifestations which could be qualified as enlightened. Among them, most important was the affirmation of the Creole personality that was mentioned earlier on in this work. Emerging from this process was the growing sentiment which can be denoted as their "Mexican-ness" as well as the possibility of their independence from the Spanish Crown. This awakened even greater interest in the study of the historical and artistic background of the cultures of ancient Mexico, as can be seen in the

House of the Count de Santiago de Calimaya. Mexico City.

literature that was produced surrounding the so-called "two stones," the Coatlicue codex and that known as the Aztec Calendar, which were discovered in 1790 while work was being undertaken to pave Mexico City's central plaza. Given this mind set, it is easy to understand the incorporation of the serpent's head in the corner of the Palace of the Count de Santiago de Calimaya.

The recovery of the Greco-Roman past is due, in part, to the activities mentioned in the foregoing, but also to the fact that from this past artists began to discover sources of inspiration as well as models. This can be noted, for example, in the glazed ceramic tiles representing the feats of Hercules on the façade of the Casa de los Muñecos (House of the Dolls), in the city of Puebla, built by the city's mayor, Agustín de Ovando y Villavicencio, in the 1790s, as well as in the relief work with mythological motifs found on the façade of the Iturbide Palace.

All of the foregoing is evidence of the Enlightenment which had swept Europe and which had also arrived in New Spain. A "Spanish Enlightenment," so to speak, which in Spain, despite the freedom promoted by this new philosophy, was adapted to the traditional cultural, social, political and religious structures.

Nevertheless, although these new ideas were reflected in the Baroque architecture of New Spain, in reality, the artistic manifestation par exellence was, as in Europe, Neoclassical architecture, that which returned to the rationalist canons of Classical architecture yet granting it a new reading. It was an artistic movement eminently international and unifying. Among the notable palaces from this epoch, of note are two which were constructed by architect Manuel Tolsá: that of the Marquis del Apartado, today housing the offices of the Ministry of Public Education, and that of the Count de Buenavista, today the Museo de San Carlos.

In the latter of the two, outstanding are two formal and spatial solutions of great importance: the semicircular entrance and the circular courtyard. To these can be added a new change in the residential architecture of the period, which was the elimination of the mezzanine and the return to the two-story house. As usual, the upper floor was the more important and, in an original solution, it was here where the columns were placed, in this case flanking the balcony, and it is also here were the ornamental elements were concentrated, principally made up of garlands and circular panels, as well as an ensemble of triangular and curved pediments which are quite reminiscent of Mannerist architecture. The house is topped by a stone balustrade adorned with urns.

The courtyard features bossed pillars on the first floor and Ionic columns adorned with garlands on the second. The house's importance is based, essentially, on its floor plan, unique in New Spain and one which recalls the palace of Charles V, in Granada.

Over three centuries, the house in New Spain suffered many spatial, architectural and artistic transformations, all of them responding to the specific, daily needs of the society which built them. They always maintained a unique personality, however, that was a reflection of the identity which this social group was refining at the time and which one day would lead them to declare their independence from Spain.

Serpent's head.
House of the Count de Santiago de Calimaya. Mexico City.

Pages 46 and 47.
House of the Count de Santiago de Calimaya. Mexico City.

The Nobility of New Spain and Their Palaces

The Nobility of New Spain and Their Palaces

Inasmuch as the [viceroy] had noted that whatever [his wife] the Marquise de Branciforte [Doña María Antonia de Godoy y Álvarez] did was quickly copied by the ladies of the colony, they invited to the palace, on one occasion, all of the aristocracy of the day, and what was their surprise to note that the Marquise was not flaunting a single pearl but, rather, a magnificent ensemble of coral. Greater was the astonishment among the guests upon hearing, from the authorized lips of the [viceroy and his wife], that pearls were no longer in fashion, only coral. In the following days, the women divested themselves of their pearls at a despicable price and bought themselves coral, while the Brancifortes, behind their backs, made a truly miraculous haul.[1]

Antonio Rubial García

This anecdote, related by Manuel Romero de Terreros, presents us with an all-to-clear picture of the characteristics of the aristocracy in the viceroyalty, or colony, of New Spain. Their ostentation was a manifestation of their desire to imitate their European counterparts, and their only available mirrors were to be found in the viceregal court and in the officials who visited from Spain. Also apparent was their need to copy the fashions and manners that they observed, the foreign pomp, so as to make themselves appear of nobility, as well as a way to negate their provincialism, their credulity and their marginality with regard to the cultural advances within the European courts. Through this behavior, we can perceive an aristocracy that needed to make clear a quality of nobility of which they could never be certain of possessing.

Such behavior could be observed within the aristocracy of New Spain beginning with the formation of the first society of *encomenderos* (the Spanish colonists who were granted indigenous laborers and/or their properties by royal decree). Friar Toribio de Motolinia made mention of the great expenditures made by the newly wealthy *encomenderos* in the construction of houses and gardens, and in

1 Romero de Terreros, *Bocetos . . .*, pp. 74-75.

La Sra. Da. Ana Maria
dela Campa Còs, Zeva-
llos Villegas, Condèsa de
Sn. Mathèo de Valparaiso
y Marquèsa del Jaràl de
Berrio.

their decoration with tapestries and other luxuries, all the while complaining bitterly about the suffering and slavery of the indigenous people to whose labor and tributes they owed such riches.[2]

2 Motolinia, *Historia . . .*, pp. 23, 165.

Not all of the *encomenderos* enjoyed such economic privileges, however, nor were they able to surround themselves with such shows of wealth. It is clear that those who accumulated the greatest fortunes were the military leaders of the conquest who got hold of the greatest and most populated of such grants from the Spanish Crown. Hernán Cortés, Francisco de Montejo, Diego de Mazariegos and, later, Francisco de Ibarra were among them. The palaces or mansions that still remain from this period, and which pertained to these men, are just a sample of the ostentatious and luxurious lifestyles which they enjoyed, an indication of elevated positions that are reminiscent of the nobility from the Middle Ages and the Renaissance.

The wealth accumulated by the first aristocracy of *encomenderos* did not, however, survive intact beyond two generations. The reduction in the indigenous population during the sixteenth century and the policies of the Crown (which tended toward limiting their privileges as well as their access to manual labor and tributes, with regard to the indigenous peoples) undermined the superior positions that they had held during the early decades of the century to such an extent that they could no longer continue to live in such a state of decadence. At any rate, some of the *encomenderos* managed to marry into the new circles that had begun, about 1570, to hold the most power, capital and expanses of land: the hacienda owners, the merchants and the officials of the royal court. These groups had become enriched by the policies of King Philip II regarding the development of mining and commerce, the growth of the cities with Spanish populations, the increased volume of supplies needed by these cities and the new social and economic conditions that were emerging within New Spain during the second half of the sixteenth century.

The new aristocracy of this landed gentry was made up, for the most part, of Creoles, as had been the second generation of *encomenderos*. Through their connections within the governments of the principal cities, this new group found a new type of position and of ostentation, which was manifested in both religious and secular festivities, as well as a means of controlling the cities' supplies of meat, grains, pulque, sugar and wool which were produced on their haciendas. Although the landowners were kept out of a number of political posts (such as viceroy, judge, governor, archbishop, and mayor), thanks to the selling of positions undertaken by the Crown, they were able to infiltrate the area of public administration to a great degree. Additionally, their wealth and social prestige allowed them to secure alliances and relationships with the viceregal bureaucracy as well as with a number of merchants.

Page 51.
Ana María de la Campa y Cos, Countess de San Mateo de Valparaíso and Marquise del Jaral de Berrio, by Andrés de Islas.
18th century. Collection of Banco Nacional de México.

Concession of the title of Marquis del Jaral de Berrio to Don Miguel de Berrio y Zaldívar.
Collection of Rodrigo Rivero Lake.

At about the end of the seventeenth century, just over one hundred families, in all of New Spain, possessed the viceroyalty's richest lands. To avoid the breaking up of their patrimonies, as well as to preserve their lineage, these landowners adhered to the institution known as the *mayorazgo*, a contract established with

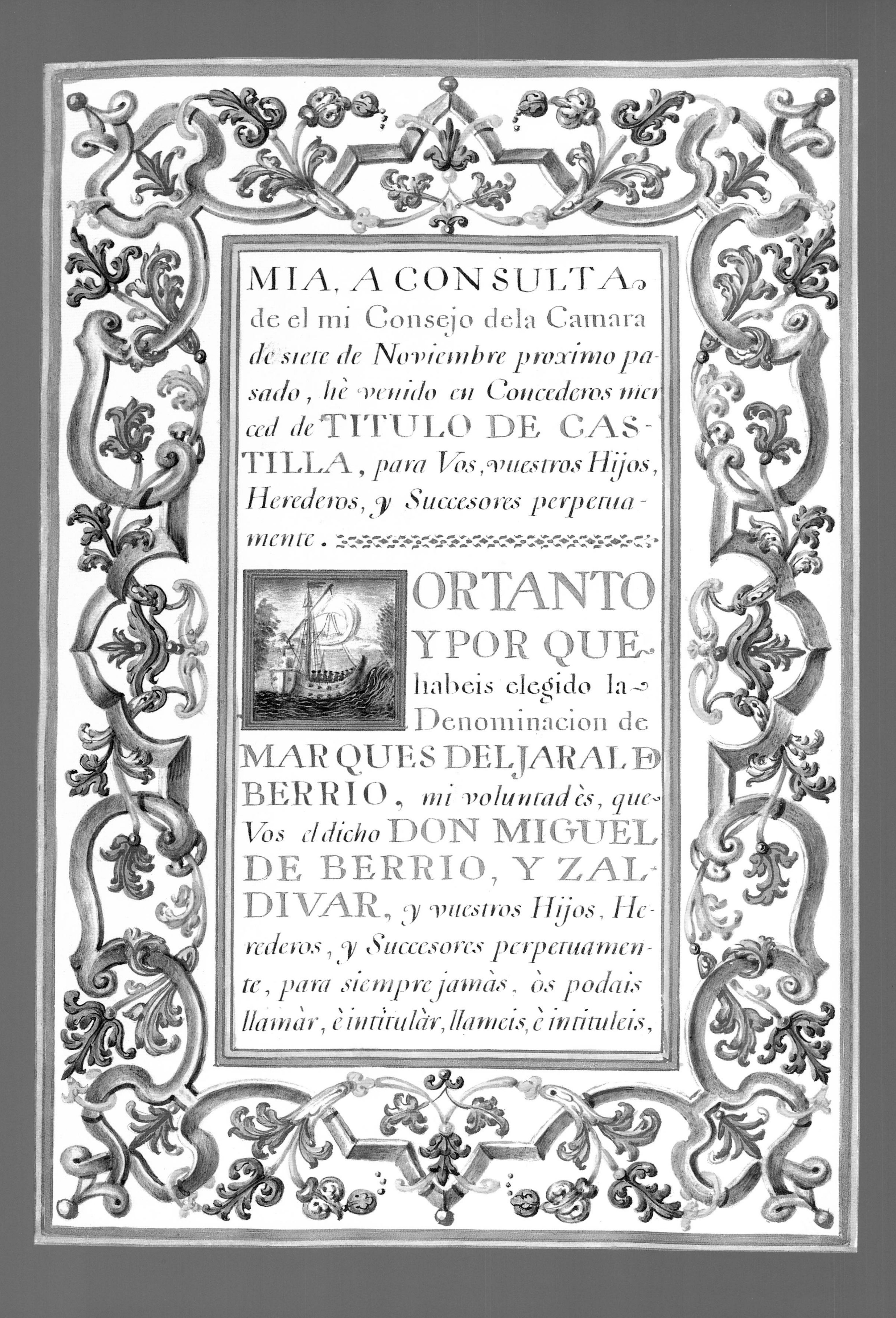

MIA, A CONSULTA
de el mi Consejo dela Camara
de siete de Noviembre proximo pa-
sado, hè venido en Concederos mer
ced de TITULO DE CAS-
TILLA, para Vos, vuestros Hijos,
Herederos, y Succesores perpetua-
mente.

PORTANTO
Y POR QUE
habeis elegido la
Denominacion de
MARQUES DEL JARAL D
BERRIO, mi voluntad ès, que
Vos el dicho DON MIGUEL
DE BERRIO, Y ZAL-
DIVAR, y vuestros Hijos, He-
rederos, y Succesores perpetuamen-
te, para siempre jamàs, òs podais
llamàr, è intitulàr, llameis, è intituleis,

the Crown by which the inheritance of the family's properties was guaranteed to the firstborn son. If, for some reason, this was not possible, his younger brothers or sisters, or the closest other relative, was granted the right. In addition to the *mayorazgo*, this group consolidated their alliances and reinforced their power and prestige through intermarriage, the *compadrazgo* (the unique relationship between parents and godparents) and the presence of numerous family members in ecclesiastical institutions. Another means of gaining status was to obtain the title of Caballero (Knight) de Santiago, de Calatrava or de Alcántara or that of Captain of Militias. One could also join a confraternity, congregation or brotherhood of notables, or bequeath a sum of money to provide dowries for orphaned girls, a convent or to pay for a series of masses to be said for one's soul in a particular church. The will, apart from assuring one a reduction of penalties in Purgatory and putting one's worldly matters and issues surrounding inheritance in order, served to right the wrongs committed during one's life, to stipulate the ceremonies to be conducted at one's funeral and, in the long run, to assure the dignity and the glory of the lineage and of the surviving members of the family.

All of the families of the landowners pertained to the same aristocracy, sharing the privileges and sentiments of an elite. They also shared a deeply rooted sense of honor, of purity of blood (proud that there were no Jews, Moslems or heathens among their ancestors), of nobility and the idea that they were worthy of their positions due to the merits of their forebears, whether through heroic feats during wartime or for services rendered to the monarch or to God. Although few of them were descendants of the Spanish aristocracy, many instead traced their lineage to the Visigoths. Among these families, however, only a few could truly be considered of high aristocracy, in terms of their great wealth and property holdings as well as for holding a title of nobility, such as count or marquis. Such titles were granted by the Crown to those who had distinguished themselves through donations to the republic or the monarchy. A title was obtained by means of a financial arrangement with the king and carried with it the obligation to pay an amount each year in taxes, in lieu of furnishing the Crown with troops. In New Spain, the number of titles that had been granted totaled eighteen by the end of the seventeenth century. A century later, however, the total had grown to over seventy, indicative of the growing need for Spain to seek funds through whatever means necessary in order to replenish the country's dwindling coffers.

Nevertheless, a title alone was not enough to be considered a nobleman of lineage. Rather, a title brought with it a complete lifestyle in which the pretensions of nobility could be established. One's public image, manifested in the fashionable attire, the jewelry, the slaves and the carriages, as well as in the rituals and the gentlemanly codes that were present in social intercourse, were complemented by family coats of arms, festive parades, hunts, magnificent parties, courtly dances and amorous courtships. Among all the symbols of noble status, doubtless one of the most representative was the ownership of a palatial mansion in Mexico City as well as a country home with a garden and orchard in what were then the outskirts of the city (San Agustín de las Cuevas de Tlalpan, San Ángel or

Certification of the coat of arms of the Marquis del Jaral de Berrio. Collection of Rodrigo Rivero Lake.

-tificacion de Armas, y en el siguiente Es-
cudete.

Parr. XIII.

POR LAS CI-
TADAS INFOR-
maciones recibidas à
instancia de nuestro inte-
resado, resulta que de la ra-
ma radicada en la referida Villa de Arciniega
de la Provincia de Alaba, dimanó Don Juan
de Zaldivar, donde y en las demas partes que

Tacubaya), along with all of the sumptuous objects that formed part of the furnishings, such as fine furniture, tapestries, paintings and luxurious objects from China and Europe.

In the early decades of the viceregal period, these mansions had the appearance of fortresses, with battlements, crenels and watchtowers, prompted by the fear of uprisings among the indigenous peoples. At the time, if one received the right to a parcel of land in the city he was obliged to build a house on it and reside there or risk losing his deed to the property. These homes were of a sober character and, at most, would sometimes feature floral decoration painted onto the masonry façades. Generally, the distribution of space resulted in two volumes, separated by a courtyard in which the chicken coop, stables and storage areas were located. Such constructions were known at the time as "pairs of houses" in that they presented a separation of the volumes housing the quarters of the "master," at the front, from that of the courtyard and service areas, in the rear. With the further establishment of the viceroyalty over the years, however, these fortified structures began to lose their militaristic character and featured façades with delicate Plateresque entrances, windows and balconies. The indigenous nobility soon began to imitate this style of house as a status symbol.[3] Over time, these palaces were remodeled thanks to the overall economic boom experienced within the kingdom and the prosperity which reached its peak during the eighteenth century. The doors and balconies were decorated with baroque ornamentation, and many of the columns and arches of the central courtyards were replaced. In spite of the modifications, many of the structures conserved the original façades – the velvety reddish and black tones of the igneous *tezontle* stone and the grayish white of the *chiluca* quarry stone used for jambs and lintels – as well as the corner niches, the gargoyles, the iron railings and the watchtowers.

3 Kubler, *Arquitectura . . .*, pp. 191 ff.

The characteristics of the home of an aristocrat in New Spain were established during the sixteenth century and were maintained over the next several centuries. The constructed spaces were distributed around a central courtyard, known as a "Castilian courtyard," a privilege enjoyed only by the upper classes. Off the central courtyard were one or two smaller ones, used as service areas and which contained fountains that were fed with potable water via a system of underground piping, an expensive extravagance also enjoyed by very few residents. This construction model was influenced by the timeless Mediterranean archetype yet also reflected characteristics from traditional Islamic architecture. On the ground floor of the palace were to be found the areas set aside as quarters for the male servants (messengers, pages, coachmen, footmen and others), the garage, the stables and storerooms. Along the side, or sides, which bordered a street were strorefronts which the owner would rent. Some of these mansions featured a mezzanine level, usually given over to quarters for servants, poor relatives of the owner or for use by the administrator of the country estate, or estates, during his sojourns in the city. One thing that European travelers were impressed by, being accustomed to double-pitched roofs, was that those of the palaces in New Spain were flat and, similar to the courtyards below, contained large pots with plants and flowers, as well as caged birds, creating veritable gardens in which to enjoy the fresh air and pass the afternoons in conversation. The area in which the family spent most of its active and restful time, however, was on the second floor, the area with the greatest amount of specialized rooms. The existence of this type of spaces was the consequence of the emergence of the concept of privacy, a criterion dictated by the "modern" age and which hadn't existed in the Middle Ages. One example are the rooms whose purposes were related to hygiene. Although the bathroom, as we know it today, did not yet exist, many of these mansions had bathtubs, sunk into the floors and decorated with mosaics, which were filled by hot water which was channeled from the kitchen. On the other hand, in an area removed from the living quarters (generally above the stables) was the space for the toilets. In it was a long platform with a series of holes, not separated by any sort of "vanity panels," which served for the elimination of one's bodily wastes as well as, in the mornings, a place in which to empty the chamber pots.

Also on the second floor, the most important space with respect to families spending time together, was the kitchen. It was not only the room in which food was prepared but, also, where the meals were consumed and in which gossip, news and rumors could be shared. Within it was to be found a long brazier upon which the traditional European, African and indigenous dishes were prepared, and where a rich and varied native cuisine was slowly taking form. This space came to life at dawn, when several servants would begin to haul up buckets of water through a shaft that led to the service courtyard below while others started the fire for the stove. The latter process was easy if any embers still remained from the night before. If not, it was necessary to strike a piece of iron against a flint stone in order to produce the sparks which would ignite a bundle of tinder. The dishes were prepared with both highly seasoned and sweet-and-sour sauces, most of the food fried in lard. Meals were complemented by desserts which contained large amounts of sugar. The accompanying beverages were fruit juices mixed with water, wine, pulque or, most commonly, hot chocolate, a veritable vice among the residents of New Spain. Made from cacao – a food, a curative and a delicacy, as well as currency – it was drunk at all hours of the day or night, generally with salt, spices, sweeteners or vanilla.[4]

4 Alberro, *Del Gachupín . . .*, pp. 75 ff.

From the seventeenth century onward, the tables in New Spain witnessed the generalized use of spoons for consuming soups and stews, and the fork for slicing food. The latter item, as had been the custom in Europe since the Renaissance, was utilized only during banquets attended by the elite. For routine meals at home, among the rich of the viceroyalty as well as the poorest, the combination of fingers and corn tortillas formed the basic utensils for eating.

During the grand, festive celebrations, the kitchen proved to be an inadequate space. Therefore, it became necessary to set up large tables in the courtyards, arcades or gardens, utilizing planks laid across sawhorses or benches and covered with tablecloths. At the head of each table was placed a makeshift counter, with various stepped levels and draped in fine fabrics, on which to set out the vessels

Page 58.
Dishware belonging to the Viceroy de Revillagigedo.
Porcelain, from the Compañía de Indias.
Private collection.

of silver and crystal. The concept of the dining room and its corresponding furniture, as a specific space within the home, did not emerge in New Spain until the middle of the eighteenth century.

Apart from the kitchen, the other spaces shared by the family were the parlor and the drawing room. In the former, close friends or relatives would be entertained. Cards and Chinese checkers were played here, embroidery was done, there was reading aloud from pious books, musical instruments were played, and it was a place for prayer in the afternoons as well as where the crèche would be placed for Christmas. The drawing room was usually furnished with a carpeted dais or platform on which the women would sit on cushions while the men sat in chairs (armchairs not appearing until much later). As the principal space where guests were received, here were to be found the most luxurious appointments in the house, including folding screens, mirrors, cornucopias, objects of crystal and silver, Chinese vases, painted or sculpted religious images and paintings of landscapes. On the principal wall of the room was nearly always to be found an oriental crucifix, of ivory, hung beneath a damask canopy. The curtains covering the windows were coordinated with the tapestries on the walls and the cushions on the dais, and the colors of same would be changed completely while the family was in mourning. The floors of the drawing room, like those of the rest of the house, were of polished wood and covered with fine oriental rugs. At night, the room was illuminated with candles accommodated in chandeliers, candlesticks and cornucopias.

The drawing room was the site for get-togethers, the chief source of diversion in this period, where there would be dancing, singing and card playing. The use of tobacco during these events was widespread, whether smoked, chewed or taken as snuff, known at the time as *rapé* and sniffed in order to provoke sneezing.

Some mansions also featured an anteroom whose walls were covered with hand-painted Chinese paper and on which was placed the family's coat of arms, portraits of its prominent members, both living and deceased, and those of daughters who had left the secular world to join convents. In the eighteenth century, the aristocrats with titles of nobility also enjoyed the privilege of placing, in a special room, a throne-like chair along with a portrait of the monarch, hung beneath a canopy. Another privilege of the aristocracy was that of maintaining a private chapel within their homes, with an altar and *retablo*, or altarpiece, a concession granted by a papal document whereby a chaplain close to the family could consecrate it. It was rare to find a library within one of these homes, the owning of books among laymen being quite uncommon. Some families, however, had collections which had been inherited, often of a professional or religious nature. On the other hand, it was common to have a study, a small room known as a *bufete* in which to write letters or make journal entries, containing a writing desk and such accessories as blotting paper, sand, pens, an inkwell and a hand bell with which to summon one of the servants.[5]

The other principal spaces devoted to the family were the bedrooms, of which each family member had his or her own, particularly in the case of the

5 Romero de Terreros, *Una casa . . .*, pp. 17 ff.

AVE
MARIA

husband and the wife. The bedrooms were where one was born and where one was to die, both acts occurring in the presence of family members and governed by religious ritual. Given the need for modesty and intimacy on the part of the mother, her bedroom was more important than any of the others. In it, a lady of the aristocracy would give birth to her children and would be attended by midwives, usually indigenous or mestizo women. Here she would carry out the activities of nursing and caring for her babies, always assisted by *chichiguas* (wet nurses) and *pilmamas* (nannies) who were generally indigenous, mestizo or mulatto. In addition to her canopy bed, folding dressing screen and chest of drawers were trunks in which were kept whalebone corsets, hoop skirts of colorful fabrics, jackets with broad sleeves and low necklines, dresses of silk and lace, and a variety of shoes, valuable objects which were treasured and passed on to her daughters. Near her bed was a dressing table, complete with the perfumes, powders and adornments appropriate to her feminine presence.

From early childhood, the women attend schools known as *de amiga* where they were instructed by elderly widows in how to become the mistress of the house. Others attended religious convents.[6] Apart from their domestic responsibilities, reading, writing and basic religious instruction, the females were taught discretion, submission, modesty, diligence and Christian piety. Although a woman was treated as a perpetual child, in the absence of a protective male she could freely exercise her rights in the making of donations and business operations, found benefices, *mayorazgos* and trusts, grant powers of attorney, prepare a will or solicit credit.[7]

Such rights could only be exercised by widows as among married women submission to the husband was absolute. In addition to his right to punish, in moderation, the members of his family, the father had the last word in the selection of a profession or a religious "vocation" as well as the future mates of his children, the latter choice often dependent on family alliances and the permanency of patrimonies and lineage. One pervasive characteristic of the elite in New Spain was that very young women married mature men, resulting in a far greater number of widows than widowers.

In addition to the legitimate children produced by the marriage, the father of an aristocratic family was allowed to shelter under his roof a numerous "clientele" of godchildren, nieces and nephews, stepchildren, "adopted" children, "protégés," and illegitimate children who often profited in terms of a higher standard of living and an occupation in addition to a mere roof over their heads and nourishment. An important element among the inhabitants of one of these palaces were the servants and the slaves, the majority of whom were quartered in the house. Some were godchildren of the owner while others had been born in the building. Cooks, servants, washerwomen and wet nurses lived in rooms adjacent to their masters while the male servants, footmen and coachmen lived on the ground floor of the mansions. Although proud of the purity of their blood and careful not to intermarry with indigenous, meztizos or Africans, the aristocracy of New Spain could not escape the strong influences exercised on them by these social sectors. The practice of magic, songs, culinary customs, traditions, legends and linguistic

6 Kubler, op. cit., p. 33.

7 Gonzalbo Aispuru, *Las mujeres . . .*, p. 151.

Pages 60 and 61.
Detail from: *Nacimiento de Santo Domingo de Guzmán*, anonymous. 18th century. Collection of the Consejo Nacional para la Cultura y las Artes - Tepozcolula, Oaxaca.

De Español y Morisca Albino, by Ramón de Torres. 18th century. Private collection.

Dª PETRA MARIA DE GUADALUPE TOMASA MONCADA Y BERRIO DE EDAD DE NUEVE AÑOS Y OCHO MESE
y Dⁿ Júan Nepomuceno María Guadalupe José Joachin Miguel Moncada y Berrio de edad de diez meſes, hijos de los Sres Dⁿ. Pedro

forms were just some of the many elements that led to a rich cultural hybrid that was slowly emerging within the walls of these grand homes.[8]

8 Rubial, *La plaza . . .*, p. 82.

These mansions shared the urban landscape with innumerable apartment buildings known as *vecindades* in which many lower- and middle–class families lived. Some contained apartments of two or three rooms while others featured small, individual rooms in which as many as two or three families lived. These buildings were often the properties of architects or pertained to convents or other religious organizations. They were frequently built along the sides of hospitals, convents or schools which rented the spaces in order to provide extra income with which to offset their operating expenses. Among these social sectors, the apartments or rooms functioned as more than mere living quarters as they were utilized as work spaces or even stores. In these *vecindades*, it was frequent that a single services area, with toilets, laundry sinks and sometimes even a stove, were used communally by all of the building's residents. With living quarters so small, dark and even unhealthy, it was common that the rooms were utilized only for sleeping, the residents spending the entire day in the street. The crowding and the promiscuity the pervaded the *vecindades* created strong bonds of solidarity and a close level of communication, but these conditions also gave birth to tensions and frequent quarrels.

There were people who lived in more precarious conditions, however, in wood or adobe huts, either within the indigenous neighborhoods or constructed against the walls of monasteries. Others, less fortunate, were forced to sleep outdoors and took shelter from the rain in the entryways of churches. In the cities of New Spain, as well as the cities of today, there existed a contrast between misery and luxury, the pearls of the aristocracy and the pleading for money by the disinherited. Christian charity, through the various organisms of assistance and the giving of alms, represented an important resource in alleviating the situation. It was the payment that religion demanded of the powerful who, in theory, were to function as the administrators of a wealth that pertained only to God.

Portrait of Petra María de Guadalupe Tomasa and Juan Nepomuceno de Moncada, anonymous.
18th century. Collection of Banco Nacional de México.

The Ancestral Mansion of the Montejo Family

Mérida, Yucatán

The Ancestral Mansion of the Montejo Family

That Yucatán is not an island nor a point that enters into the sea as many thought, rather solid ground and that they confused it for the Point of Cotoch which juts into the sea forming the Bahía de la Ascensión facing the Golfo Dulce and, for the point that in this other part, toward Mexico, forms the Desconocido [Bay] before arriving in Campeche, or for the extension of the lagoons that meet the sea at Puerto Real and Dos Bocas.

That it is very flat and free of jagged mountains and that therefore it wasn't discovered by ship until very near (the coast), except between Campeche and Champotón where one can see some low hills and a promontory which they call those of the demons.[1]

Mayte Sánchez Lozano

With these words, Friar Diego de Landa begins his work and calls attention to the fact that the Yucatán had been correctly defined. Nearly all of those who first came to this continent wrongly believed that it was an island, an error that was committed for many years, until well into the sixteenth century when, after being thoroughly explored, and later conquered and colonized by Don Francisco de Montejo, his son and his nephew, it became accepted that, in reality, it was a peninsula.

This peninsula, having been the first land discovered west of the island of Cuba, conserved its original name, and this same name was utilized to identify all the lands which were later to be known as "New Spain."

The name "Yucatán" has been the subject of much controversy with regard to its etymology and whether or not it pertained to the indigenous language. It is most probably not a Mayan word but, rather, an adulteration of other Mayan words, unconsciously distorted by the conquistadors, in particular by Francisco Hernández de Córdoba who was the first official explorer of the territory that today forms part of Mexico and who was commissioned to do so by the governor of Cuba at the time, Diego Velázquez.

1 Landa, *Relación* . . . , p. 7.

It was in the Yucatán where, by order of Pope Leo X, the first bishopric in New Spain was established. The act was no more than honorary, however, in that not only were the boundaries of the diocese not defined nor an episcopal seat determined, but there was not even a bishop designated to take up the post. It wasn't until 1523 when the Bishop and the Emperor made a formal petition to the Holy See that the boundaries be determined, leaving it to Pope Clement VII to delimit the territory and jurisdiction of what was named the Bishopric of Yucatán y Santa María de los Remedios. Ironically, the Yucatán Peninsula was excluded from this diocese because, at that point in time, the area was not yet under the domination of the Spanish king. Friar Julián Garcés then dropped the title of Bishop of Yucatán and took that of Bishop of Tlaxcala. The edict was signed in Granada granting him the title of Bishop Carolense. In 1527, he arrived in New Spain and remained in his post until his death in 1542.

When the Spanish arrived on the peninsula, they found no centralized indigenous government. Rather, there existed nineteen independent chieftains who were mistrustful of each other. They were headed by a chieftain known as Batab or Batabi-uinic, a prestigious title which denoted his honor and his just and righteous conduct. The area in which the city of Mérida was later to be located pertained to the territory of Chakan which, in the Mayan language, signified meadow, savanna or plateau. Its capital was Causel and here were found the ruins of the ancient city of T'Hó. The principal chieftain was the Batab Euan, a prestigious personage not only for his character as supreme priest but for his talent and capacity for governing.

By order of the king, the titles of explorer, pacifier, conquistador and colonizer were granted to Governor Don Francisco de Montejo, nicknamed "the old man," who later conferred these titles on his son, Francisco de Montejo León, known as "the boy," and the son of his sister María, Francisco de Montejo, known as "the nephew," who together took on the difficult task of subjugating the Yucatán.

Don Francisco de Montejo, "the old man," came from a family of illustrious noblemen in Spain. Born in Salamanca in the 1460s, his father's family came from the Villa de Montejo, in Segovia. This accounts for his surname and for the three golden stars that decorate his coat of arms. Bernal Díaz del Castillo notes:

[H]e was of about medium height, a body of robust musculature, of very good spirit, intrepid, very consistent in his projects and in his decisions, daring. He had a cheerful and festive temperament, sharing joviality with his friends. He knew how to guess the intentions of his enemies, managing to sidestep them and never failing to be conscious of the means. He expressed himself easily, judging by his social manner he very much liked to develop businesses and had good knowledge of the keys that must be used in the designs of humanity. He greatly liked to work and was exceedingly intriguing. He was arrogant and of great ambitions. Greatly given over to dreaming and tenacious with his adversaries. He spent money even when he no longer had any, bordering on a lack of honesty and was, however, very fond of business and of great diplomatic aptitudes.[2]

2 Chamberlain, *Conquista . . .*, p. 32.

Knowledge about the life of Francisco de Montejo, "the old man," dates to about 1513-14 when he joined Pedrarías Dávila in the conquest of Panama. He acted in an official capacity when he was sent to Santo Domingo to recruit more men to serve in the fighting in Panama. As he felt that his services were not sufficiently rewarded, however, he and a number of his companions joined Diego Velázquez in the conquest of Cuba and was very soon rewarded with *encomiendas* (properties and indigenous laborers granted Spanish colonists by royal decree) which served to develop his haciendas. At the beginning of the sixteenth century, he had met Doña Ana de León, in Seville, the daughter of nobility, and shortly after 1508 they had a son who was to become known as Francisco Montejo León, "the boy." Don Francisco was ambitious and had good commercial sense. He managed his properties well and planned to become an investor in the Conquest. Meanwhile he waited patiently for the most auspicious moment to do so.

When he learned that there were new opportunities in the exploration and conquest of the West, in 1518, he enlisted in the expedition by Juan de Grijalva. It should be pointed out here that all of the activities involving conquest and occupation were financed exclusively by private parties, although in the name of the king. The only intervention by the Crown was in the granting of licenses or contracts when the applicants demonstrated the required abilities as well as the prestige and resources necessary to carry out the missions. As such, Montejo spent a considerable sum of his own money in preparing for this second expedition, recruiting soldiers and sailors, and provisioning a ship that he was then named to command. This was the first expedition to establish friendly contact with the indigenous people of the Yucatán Peninsula.

The following year, he accompanied Hernán Cortés who sent him, with two small ships, to reconnoiter the coast north of Veracruz in order to determine an adequate site upon which to establish a permanent settlement. This turned out to be Villa Rica de la Vera Cruz, and Montejo became one of the first heads of local government on land which pertained to New Spain. Months later, Cortés chose him, along with Alonso Hernández Portocarrero, to be his representative before the Crown in defending his rights to exercise supreme authority in the new territories, in opposition to the pretensions of Velázquez. He was also charged with transporting the magnificent treasure of gold, silver, jewels and exotic feathers, a gift from Cortés to the Emperor. So as not to fall into the hands of the governor of Cuba, Montejo traced a new route and undertook the first crossing via the Bahama Channel, which was later to become the regular route from the Americas to Spain. This assignment was repeated twice, earning him enormous prestige for his obvious talent, honesty and diplomatic tact.

In 1526, Montejo was in Granada with Charles V. He saw his opportunity and decided to present the king with his independent project for the conquest and colonization of the Yucatán. His point of view toward the natives was basically humanitarian, and he was interested in their well-being as a true colonizer and administrator more than as a warrior and conqueror. As a good Spaniard and Christian, he represented the core of the Crown's policies and was so persuasive

that he quickly obtained the approval of the young king and that of the Council of the Indies. On December 8, 1526, the Crown granted him an exclusive privilege, or contract, leaving in his hands the conquest of the Yucatán. The document stipulated that Montejo should continue the exploration of the "islands" of Yucatán and Cozumel and authorized him to conquer and colonize these lands at his own expense, with no cost to the Crown, and with no more personal reward than that stipulated in his contract.[3]

3 Ibid., p. 22.

As Montejo had already provided services to the Crown, and it was hoped that he would be of further service in the future, he was granted the title and post, in perpetuity, of Governor of Yucatán and Captain General of the province, with full civil and military authority, as well as that of Chief Magistrate of Yucatán and commander of the two fortresses that were to be built in the province. Additionally, as a form of compensation to Montejo, his heirs and successors for the expenditures that they would be required to make, he was granted, in perpetuity, 4% of all income produced from any and all sources in the Yucatán and an exemption from the import and export duties for merchandise and provisions of all types including domestic animals, munitions, etc., as well as a license to import cattle from the West Indies without limitation.

All those who accompanied Montejo on his first expedition and who stayed on as colonists were to be exempt for five years from the payment of duties and the tax placed on salt. Additionally, they were to be granted land on which to develop their haciendas as well as two lots on which to construct their houses which, after five years, would convert into private property. Furthermore, the Yucatán was to enjoy all of the other privileges, exemptions and benefits that existed in other provinces in the Indies. To preserve these privileges, it was incumbent on Montejo that no person considered undesirable should be allowed entrance into the Yucatán, among them criminals, Jews, Moors, converts and those of dubious loyalty or orthodoxy.

It was incorporated into Montejo's concession, in its totality, an important Royal Ordinance of November 17, 1526, which specified the objectives of the conquest, regulated the relations with the Indians and established the norms for attracting the inhabitants of the New World to the Church (principal desire of the Crown) and under the dominion of the Spanish monarch. This ordinance was the result of a prolonged deliberation on the part of the principal Spanish officials, jurists and ecclesiastics and represented an important step in the policies of the Crown. It was in the agreements with Montejo that the royal ordinances were incorporated for the first time, he having been the first Governor scrupulously admonished so that he be subject to the letter and the spirit of said ordinances. It was proclaimed that the intention of the Crown of Castile was to attract the natives of the New World to loyalty and the true faith through knowledge and charitable treatment, and later to protect them against abuses, unjust captivity and 'destruction'. It

AMORDEI

declared that the Indians should be considered as free beings and that under no circumstances should they be obligated by the Spanish to work against their will or without compensation. All of the natives enslaved unjustly and against the law should be set free.[4]

4 Ibid., p. 24.

The foregoing reveals the true and benevolent intentions of the Sovereign of Castile toward the natives of this region, additionally ordering that two members of the regular or secular clergy, fully suitable, should always accompany any expedition of commerce, discovery, conquest or colonization and should strive with all determination to safeguard the well-being of the natives and inform the Crown of any violation of the stipulations of the ordinances. The agreements and ordinances applicable to Montejo speak of the realism of the Spain of the period and of its new nationalism, with its advanced theories in the areas of politics, economics and religion. Apart from its ongoing crusade, the Crown promoted the conquest of new territories as the standard bearer of the Catholic faith, first for God and then for King, consecrating itself, historically, as the most Catholic of nations and making the Spaniard the most loyal of subjects.

With the sale of his properties in Salamanca, as well as diverse loans and the additional contributions (which must have been great) by Doña Beatriz Álvarez de Herrera, a rich widow and a native of Seville, who was soon to become his wife, Montejo put together enough money to acquire four good ships and the provisions necessary to set sail with more than 250 men. When they arrived on the peninsula, they founded Salamanca de Campeche, three leagues from Champotón, establishing their initial base of operations. Here they were received peacefully by the natives of the area who were later gathered together by the Governor so that he might inform them of the intentions of his voyage and his sojourn in these lands.

[T]hen with an interpreter that we brought, our Governor tried to make them understand that we did not come to kill, hurt or rob them, rather to make them understand how there is a God in Heaven, whom all Spaniards revere and how Your Majesty is on the earth, whom all Spaniards obey, venerate and honor, that they try to make way for the priests who will preach the Holy Gospel, and that to our Governor in the name of Your Majesty they recognize his dominion and that we pardon them for all of the deaths and damage that they have caused us; that from here onward in your Royal Name we will defend them from their enemies if they wish . . .[5]

5 Ibid., p. 102.

The conquest of the Yucatán may be divided into two distinct periods. The first, prior to 1535, involved the undertakings directed by Montejo himself in the occupation of the province. These efforts ended in failure due to the fact that the indigenous people harassed him continually, laying waste to his outposts and not submitting so easily to either the new owners or to God, problems which led Montejo to abandon his attempts, not returning to the Yucatán until 1546.

In his absence, his son, "the boy," in command of "the nephew" and other captains, virtually completed the conquest, pacification and colonization of the peninsula.

In 1542, "the boy" decided that T'Hó would be the best site on which to found the capital of the province.[6] It was a site refreshed by breezes, pleasant, surrounded by abundant pasture land as well as a rich and flourishing population that would aid in its construction and maintenance. At the center of the settlement were five large, high hills formed from loose stones covered with earth. Each had served as the foundation for an ancient building whose ruins could still be seen through the trees and brush that had sprung up among them during their prolonged abandonment. The explorers contemplated these grandiose ruins in astonishment, intrigued by what they might have been. These were the first such ruins they had seen since leaving their native Spain and evoked memories of the Roman ruins scattered around the city of Mérida, in the Extremadura region of Spain. As such, they named the new capital Mérida de Yucatán. Its foundation included a city council and a regiment. The new city included sixty Spanish families and 300 indigenous residents, and was founded "in honor and reverence of the Incarnation for His holy service . . . ." Immediately, city officials were named, among them conquistadors of the region, with a variety of administrative and judicial functions, each presented with a baton as a symbol of their dignity. Once the municipal government had been installed, work began on laying out the city, all agreeing that there should be a central plaza and locating it at the site of the large hill on which had stood the indigenous temple, leveling it in such a way that it formed a square. From the plaza were to initiate the four principal streets and around it were to be built public arcades for the comfort of merchants and customers. Of the parcels of land surrounding the plaza, that on the east side was reserved for the construction of the cathedral church, as far as we know the only cathedral structure in the viceroyalty of New Spain which was completed in the sixteenth century. The north side was given over to the royal house and the residence of the governor while the west side was destined for the offices of the city government and the councilmen. The south side was reserved for Montejo, "the boy," where he might build a residence for his father. The streets were to be broad and straight so that citizens might travel them with horses, wagons and other animals, and so that they better serve in defending against attacks by native groups.

The secondary streets were laid out so as to form blocks, each one containing four lots. The plan was drawn up and signed by Don Francisco de Montejo himself, after which it was delivered to city hall to be stored in the archives. On the plan, each of the lots is noted with the name of the head of the household or the conquistador to whom it had been granted. Such a grant brought along with it the obligation to construct a house with a good foundation and masonry walls, with large courtyards for animals and service facilities. The houses were constructed close together so as to better serve in defending them in the case of an attack by the natives. Soon the city began to spread out beyond the original plan and the streets began to display a rather original nomenclature given that on every corner, rather than a name, was to be found the figure of an animal or another type of symbol allusive to some

6 López de Cogolludo, *Historia . . .*, vol. I, p. 219. Cogolludo swears to having seen and read the original decree of the foundation and that it was dated January 6, 1542, although a councilman of the city of Mérida, in 1579, stated that the date of the foundation was February 6, 1542.

public event. Each of these evocative elements was executed in bas-relief or placed within a niche. Today, we can still appreciate two of them *in situ*: that of the elephant an another of a human figure known as a *monifato*.

The original city was laid out as comprising twenty blocks with a carefully marked perimeter which featured seven majestic arches, luxurious monuments of great height. The arches Dragones, Puente and San Juan are examples that still exist today and which provide us with an image of the sixteenth century.

The city was divided into four districts: San Sebastián, to the south, for the Spaniards; Santiago y Santa Catalina, to the west, for the indigenous Mayans, an area they had occupied in the original city of T'Hó; San Cristóbal, to the east, for the indigenous people that Montejo had brought from his *encomienda* at Atzcapotzalco; and Santa Lucia y Santa Ana, to the north, for the blacks and the mulattos. It is believed that construction on the ancestral home of the Montejo family began immediately after the founding of the city. This is due to the fact that the only known date with respect to the construction appears in the inscription carved in stone near the top of the façade, between the two lions. It reads: "This work was ordered by Governor Don Francisco de Montejo year MDXLIX." Most probably, this was the year in which the construction was terminated.

The last mission that "the old man" undertook in the New World was the transportation of a shipment of gold and silver from the royal treasury. He was given detailed instructions in an order from Viceroy Mendoza, dated October 26, 1550, in the city of Cholula. Enjoying the confidence of the government of the viceroyalty, this man, now elderly, arrived in Spain having served his country and his king. He died three years later in his native Salamanca.

The mansion of the Montejo family once occupied four lots, but today only the façade remains. It is, however, doubtless the most valuable jewel of civil architectural from the sixteenth century in all of the Americas. It is worth noting here the few other mansions from said century that still remain standing. In San Cristóbal de las Casas is that which was once the residence of the city's magistrate, Diego de Mazariegos, and that of Andrés de la Tobilla, although both of these are much simpler in design. In the city of Puebla are that known as "The House of the One Who Killed the Animal" and that of the Dean of the Cathedral of Puebla, as well as part of what once was the public granary. Another is found in Tlaxcala, the Palace of Government. In the city of Oaxaca there are several houses from the sixteenth century although they are quite sober, and in Guadalajara there remain some jambs and lintels which resemble those in Puebla. One more of note can be found in Patzcuaro.

A description of the formal repertoire of the Montejo house, while doubtless the most magnificent monument from the period, is difficult to reconstruct. In addition to the difficulties in locating information within public archives, a number of documents have been scattered among private collectors. Thanks to Don Ignacio Rubio Mañé, however, who through difficult and meticulous effort located the majority of the data pertaining to parish archives as well as records found in the archives of the city of Mérida and the General Archive of the Nation,

in Mexico City, it has been possible to assemble trustworthy information.

Another factor aggravating our appreciation of the mansion is that it has suffered numerous modifications, the victim of the tastes of its successive owners and the architectural and decorative fashions of the various periods during its more than four centuries of existence.

Upon the death of Governor Montejo, his widow, Doña Beatriz de Herrera, continued to reside there for a short time. She then moved to the capital of New Spain, Mexico City, where she died in 1560. The property was inherited by "the boy" Montejo who lived there until his death in 1565, leaving behind a magnificent reputation which was never to be denigrated. He also left a fabulous amount of debts, however, which led to the house being put up for auction. Fortunately, his wife, Doña Andrea del Castillo, was able to rescue the house from the auction and continued to live there, founding a *mayorazgo* (a contract established with the Crown by which the inheritance of the family's properties was guaranteed to the firstborn son) for her descendants.[7]

7 Rubio Mañé, *La Casa . . .*, pp. 23-116. This resource provides greater detail regarding the subsequent owners of the Montejo home.

Description of the Façade

The façade of the ancestral home of the Montejo family is comprised of two levels, topped by a pediment of a classical shape. The first level is organized around the straight lines of the entrance portal which opens onto the public plaza. Staggered ashlars rise from the base of the façade, at each end, whose recesses and projections add luster to the two slim, fluted columns with composite capitals. These are a magnificent complement to their corresponding antas, composite and paneled, and are mounted on pedestals and placed in such a way as to dictate the shape of the cornice. The ornamental frame that surrounds the doorway is formed by panels sculpted with animal and vegetal motifs in high relief and at the center, within circles and scalloped molding, are two human heads. On the lintel are two panels, one on each side of the keystone, each of which holds an imaginary bird which jealously guards a tablet with an inscription. The one on the left reads "AMOR DEI" and the one on the right "VINCIT" ("The love of God conquers all"). In each corner is a panel with a sculpted head. The one on the left is a bearded man whose head is covered by a type of helmet. To the right is a woman who is wearing a crown. Most notable on the first level is the keystone of the architrave. It features a human figure who appears to be elderly. He is wearing lambskin and is bent over, seemingly in order to bear on his back the weight of the corbel which supports the balcony. The composite capitals feature acanthus leaves and the heads of small children, as well as rams' horns. The columns support the entablature which includes an architrave ornamented with round and vertical cavities. The frieze features imaginary animals and just above each of the columns are three cherubs. At the center there is a structure resembling a pedestal that serves to ornament the cornice with eight cherubs whose faces exhibit a variety of expressions. The cornice juts out considerably, faithfully following the lines of

the structure beneath it. It is adorned with dentils, and what appear to be flower buds or hanging fruit. From here we are drawn to the upper level.

The second level, or volume, contains two small pedestals which seem to be a continuation of the capitals of the columns below. Each is ornamented with a bearded face accompanied by a halberd, the weapon of the royal ensigns, and above each head is the face of a child. Standing on each pedestal is a representation of a savage-looking man who holds a trunk-like club with one arm, reminiscent of the *bastos* in the deck of Spanish playing cards. The doorway at the center which opens onto the balcony features a monolithic frame adorned with medallions at the corners and corbel-like pairs of small heads. The area of frame surrounding this is bossed with button-like ornaments in high relief set into depressions in the frame, the stones containing them carved into irregular blocks. To each side of the doorway, resting on the cornice, is a fluted pedestal upon which is a soldier. They stand with each of their feet resting on the sorrowful head of a victim, all of whom seem to be exhaling cries of anguish. These bearded conquistadors bear the battle gear of the period: breastplate, helmet, halberd in one hand and a sword in the other. They stand against counterpilasters with capitals that appear to contain griffins. At the center of each are the anagrams "IHS" (Jesus), on the left, and "MA" (Mary), on the right. Thick foliage, which seems to include bells rather than fruit, surrounds the coat of arms of the Montejo family and covers the entire panel above the doorway. Above and protecting the coat of arms is a beautiful helmet, facing directly forward, with an eagle for a crest, also facing forward.

The coat of arms is composed of four quarters and is a representation of the following: At the upper left is a quartered shield, the coat of arms conceded to Governor Montejo by Charles V, including the coat of arms of his lineage and that of his merits, forming a veritable allegory. In the upper left section of this quarter is an isle against whose rose-colored background is a golden lion and some scattered particles of gold. In the upper right is a golden castle with three red flags, constructed on solid ground along a coast. In the lower left are seven round "loaves" of gold against a blue background, and in the lower right five blue flags against a gold background. Along the edge are thirteen golden stars against a red background. The symbolism is representative various events, for example the isle represents the place where Montejo first planted the Spanish flag on the Isla de Sacrificios. The golden castle and the red flags represent the strength of the indigenous peoples. The seven loaves of gold, the gold received from the natives when Montejo reached the Banderas River. The five blue flags recall those he received from the natives when he disembarked on the coast of Veracruz.

The second quarter, to the upper right, is divided vertically. To the left appear two large figures with raised handles that terminate in serpents heads surrounded by twelve smaller ones. To the right is an oak tree and two wolves passant representing the heraldry of the Herrera y Ayala family, the family of Beatriz de Herrera, wife of Don Francisco, "the old man."

The third quarter, to the lower left, is also divided vertically. To the left is another oak tree and a wolf passant. To the right are nine poplar leaves, arranged

in groups of three, adorned with saltires. This quarter corresponds to the coat of arms of the Álvarez de Castañeda family, predecessors of Montejo and to which his father-in-law also belonged.

Finally, the quarter in the lower right contains thirteen stars with a border comprised of a Franciscan girdle against a bright red background, the original coat of arms of the Montejo family.

The upper cornice features molding with dentils and a frieze with animal motifs among which are to be found three human heads, a male at the center and what appear to be females on either side. This cornice, which divides the upper floor from the pediment, runs along the entire front of the façade and is ornamented with vegetal forms. The façade is topped by a triangular pediment whose tympanum is ornamented with two lions rampant that proudly frame an inscription which is crowned by the presence of the head of a bearded man. It reads: "This work was ordered by Governor Don Francisco de Montejo year MDXLIX."

The house of the Montejo family is of the Plateresque style, a term that was utilized for the first time in the seventeenth century and encompassed all the works executed in architecture, the decorative arts and furniture design developed in Spain based on the manner and style of the exquisite marvels created by the silversmiths. This style flourished between 1480 and 1560 and emerged as an expression of the new Spanish nationalism promoted by the Catholic Kings and their ministers, and the cardinals Cisneros and Mendoza. It is the result of the combination of three artistic traditions: the Gothic, Italian Renaissance and Moorish. As an ornamental novelty, it was enthusiastically adopted in civil architecture. It was brought to the New World by the conquistadors in order to add a touch of artistic grace to their austere mansions. Constructed like fortified castles, the style had to be adapted to new types of windows and doors, resulting in pilasters with dense foliage, medallions with faces in high relief, and other refinements that the noble and the rich in Spain were employing to adorn their lordly houses. Thus, the private residences in the New World, such as that of the Montejo family, today allow us the opportunity to observe and appreciate the best examples of the Plateresque style from the countries in the Americas in which the Spanish extended their influence. Cogolludo, Molina Solís, Rubio Mañé and Stephens, each an indisputable authority on the subject, all coincide in affirming that the stone that was carved was from the ancient Mayan temple that had crowned the tallest of the hills of what once had been the city of Ichcanzihó, and that the sculpting was carried out by Mayan craftsmen who will forever remain anonymous. The model and design are obviously based on the Plateresque style from Spain and the iconographic symbols are rich in possible interpretations. The central figure of the composition is the elderly man who bears the weight of the balcony on his back. For Manuel Toussaint, he represents the architect of the mansion, recalling the posture of the famous master Mateo who is to be found on the central pillar of the Portico de la Gloria in Santiago de Compostela. In this position, he supports the entire weight of the structure. It rests upon him and depends upon him.

For Guillermina Vázquez it constitutes the central symbol of the entire iconographic program:

"We have identified this figure as the mythological hero Hercules, in one of his twelve prodigious labors. With it Montejo comes to place himself as the new American Hercules, just as Cortés had been in New Spain. The gallant spirit that had guided the undertakings of the conquistadors brought them to express themselves in the language of mythology, hoping in this way to legitimize the conquest, since Hercules had come to be considered the representation of the king of Spain. In those lands the undertakings of a monarch were always identified with the labors of Hercules."[8]

8 Vázquez, "Una aproximación . . . ," p. 163.

During the sixteenth century, Hercules was perhaps the most widely represented personage in civil as well as religious architecture, a result of the humanist fervor of the Renaissance which contributed greatly to such diffusion.

Another interesting element are the human faces which appear on the upper corners of the door frame on the ground floor. They may represent Don Francisco de Montejo, "the old man," and his wife, Doña Beatriz de Herrera, who it should be remembered contributed considerable sums of money toward the conquest and colonization of the Yucatán. Additionally, one might identify Don Francisco "the boy" as the figure at the center of the frieze on the upper floor since it was he who actually carried out the exploration, pacification and colonization, as well as the one who chose the most appropriate site for the new city.

To one side of each of the conquistadors above the entrance, on the upper level of the façade, is a being of intriguing identity. These are the "wild men." They are bearded and nude, covered with thick hair, and each is armed with a club or cudgel. The outstanding ethnologist Roger Bartra, in his book *Wild Men in the Looking Glass*, offers this with reference to the conquistadors:

My first impression upon observing the wild Europeans who arrived in America was that these coarse conquistadors had brought their own savagery so as to avoid that their ego dissolve in the extraordinary otherness that they were discovering. It seemed as though the Europeans had to temper the voices of their identities upon remembering that the Other – their alter egos – had always existed and with them they could avoid falling into the whirlwind of the authentic otherness that surrounded them.[9]

9 Bartra, *El Salvaje . . .* , p. 13.

This myth is far-reaching, of multiple interpretations and for that very reason difficult to explain since each epoch, says Bartra,

elaborates its own wild men with their peculiarities and specialties. If the context that surrounds them changes, they are rescued by a new cultural sensibility in that this myth holds an immense wealth of metaphors which develop multiple meanings. From the modern perspective, it has been said that the myth of the wild man is an expression of the counterpoint between culture and nature, granting coherence to the long chain of being wild.[10]

10 Ibid., p. 193.

Bartra concludes his book with a line that seems highly revealing: "This Western obsession with the Other, as an inner experience and as a way of defining the I, has veiled the presence of other voices: the Other has hidden the other."[11]

11 Ibid., p. 197.

When Inmobiliaria Banamex acquired the mansion, they undertook a conscientious study of the building, in March of 1981, with a view toward its restoration. The project, authorized by the División de Monumentos Históricos of the Instituto Nacional de Antropología e Historia, encompassed the preservation of the house, adapting it to its life as the home of banking offices, including the demolition of a number of courtyards resulting from later interventions.

The first surprise came while investigating the pilasters from the nineteenth century in an arcade on the ground floor. Architect Roberto Ancona Riestra, of the aforementioned Division of Historic Monuments, located an iron rainwater down spout in appalling condition and, upon removing it, he discovered a stone column of the Doric order which was dated to the sixteenth century. After this find, the remaining pilasters were checked. The plaster was removed from one of the arches and beneath it was discovered another, original arch. These finds led to a profound archaeological investigation utilizing excavation techniques based on test borings in the floors in order to determine their original levels, the construction materials employed, the design and original layout, the modifications made to spaces such as doors, windows, niches and openings now filled in, the precise location of the original staircase, the original color scheme, the original design of the arcades from the sixteenth century and their support columns and, finally, to attempt to define the size of the original house.

The work was completed successfully and the findings showed that not only the façade had been conserved but, also, a good number of other elements from the sixteenth century, although covered over or altered. It would seem that the oldest part of the mansion corresponds to the entire northern volume and part of the western volume, whose courtyard is framed by an arcade composed of eight very slim Doric columns. The level of the original floor was a good deal lower. The thickness of the original walls was found to be only about 1.25 m and there had been a mouth of a well in the central courtyard. At the point of this corner, just above the area of the entrance from the sixteenth century, there was a small area on the upper floor which is believed to have been the bedroom of Gov. Montejo, with an adjoining room, to the south, which served as a vestibule and provided access to the staircase. This staircase was located to the east of the entrance lobby, as evidenced by the discovery of the remains of decorative mural painting, featuring arabesques (executed with stencils or stamps) on the walls of both floors which follow the line of the staircase, tracing the placement of the flights and landings.

The house of the Montejo family in the city of Mérida, Yucatán, is a superior work which makes patent the spirited endeavors of a family of conquistadors, crowned with the triumph of immortality.

THE HOUSE OF THE DIEZMO

MORELIA, MICHOACAN

The House of the Diezmo

It has a singular effect, after traveling for some days through a wild country, seeing nothing but a solitary hacienda, or an Indian hut, to enter a fine city like Morelia, which seems to have started up as by magic in the midst of the wilderness, yet bearing all the traces of a venerable old age.[1]

Nelly Sigaut

A city is a fabric of time and space in which are interwoven the dreams of the diverse human groups which construct it and modify it through the ongoing consolidation of their different projects. As such, according to Marsilio Ficino, the concept that guides this work is that *the city is not made of stone, rather of men.* This concept implies a methodological option that makes impossible the study of a building exclusively from the architectural point of view, in terms of the description of the stylistic and spatial elements, without the added perspective of its own "life history." The objective is to try to achieve that the house reveal something of its secrets, although perhaps we may not manage to fully penetrate its intimacy.

The House of the Diezmo (Casa del Diezmo), as the building which houses a branch of Banco Nacional de México in Morelia is known, is a structure of considerable importance in the life of the community. It has the characteristics of what can be referred to as *relevant architecture* in that due to its historical and artistic value, the architecture defends itself. Here it is necessary to clarify that these historical and aesthetic values, in reality, form a whole. In fact, the historical value of a monument includes the consideration of its form as subject to an aesthetic valuation.[2]

This type of building, situated in the historic center of the city, one block from both the Cathedral and the Palace of Government, along the city's principal avenue – at the time, Real, later, Nacional, and today, Madero – houses which bear names and surnames, apart from being relevant have acquired the characteristics of symbols as well as points of reference for the inhabitants of the city, for their spatial organization or for the determination of urban growth,

1 Calderón de la Barca, *Life . . .*, p. 478.

2 Argan, *Historia . . .*, p. 217.

consolidating an order according to which the city is organized. This order is expressed through these signs, which can be read, such as the case of the house we are going to visit, in terms of its spaces and its history.

To the Rhythm of Chisels and Bells

In spite of its competition with Pátzcuaro in becoming the capital of the province, a matter which wasn't resolved until the eighteenth century, and the prosperity of other, secondary cities and towns from the middle of the seventeenth century onward, Michoacán society was dominated by the city known at the time as Valladolid.[3] The Augustinian historian Mathías de Escobar pointed out that while Pátzcuaro demonstrated "the demeanor of a town" Valladolid boasted "courtly airs."

3 See: Herrejón Peredo, *Los orígenes* . . . .

It is the latter which became the seat of the bishopric of Michoacán, the richest in New Spain (apart from the archbishopric of Mexico City), which concentrated within its borders three quarters of the ranches and half of the haciendas and mines in New Spain. As a point of reference, apart from the current states of Guanajuato and Michoacán, the bishopric included, at its height, parts of the present-day states of Nuevo León, Tamaulipas, San Luis Potosí, Colima, Guerrero and Jalisco.[4]

4 Pastor and Romero Frizzi, "Expansión . . . ," vol.II, pp. 162-191. With particular respect to the borders and extension of the Bishopric of Michoacán, see: Mazín, *El Gran Michoacán*.

The rhythm of Valladolid was marked by church bells accompanied by the sounds of chisels carving the quarry stone with which to construct volumes for God and for man. In fact, according to a report from the early seventeenth century, in Valladolid they were

> *making many houses and sumptuous buildings*
> *and so it is very civilized and there are within it*
> *220 houses and 820 heads of households which*
> *have 465 children, and 1116 servants, 229 slaves*
> *and on the outskirts, twelve towns in which there*
> *are more that a thousand Indians . . . .*[5]

5 Lemoine, "Documentos . . . ," pp. 96-97.

Perhaps these houses began to suffer from the materials employed in their construction, about the middle of the seventeenth century, when Don Gonzalo de Paz y Toledo, Councilman of Valladolid, Steward of the convent of nuns of Santa Catalina de Siena, and Chief Auditor of the Cathedral, together with his wife, Antonia de Doramás, decided to establish themselves in the city, purchasing a lot that contained a structure in a ruinous state which they ordered demolished.[6] It is on this spot where, today, stands the house which is the subject of this text.

6 Ibarrola Arriaga, *Familias* . . . , p. 125. All of the information regarding the early years of the house, until it became the House of the Diezmo, was culled from this book.

For Creoles such as Paz y Toledo, a descendant of conquistador Hernán Cortés, on his father's side, and of the Count de Oropesa, on his mother's side, a municipal post was one of the few public offices to which he could aspire. As such, the sale of such posts became a common practice throughout nearly the entire period of the viceroyalty of New Spain, although only the Spanish and the richest of the Creoles were in a position to purchase them. The deposits that had to be paid for such a post, as well as the inventories of the properties of some of these councilmen, demonstrate that they were individuals of great economic solvency.[7]

7 Juárez Nieto, *El Clero . . .*, pp. 69-75.

On December 20, 1660, Paz y Toledo and his wife sold the property, having decided to return to live in Pátzcuaro, to Pedro Marín de Villaseñor, priest of the Sagrario of the Cathedral of Valladolid and Steward of its revenues. In the contract, certified by the notary Sebastián Gutiérrez de Aragón, the couple stated that they would sell the house which they built "from the foundation up," located "on the street which runs from the Central Plaza toward the town of Charo on the route to Mexico City, across from the episcopal houses," for the amount of $3,500 pesos in common gold.[8]

8 Ibid., p. 126.

The price paid by the priest Marín speaks of the importance of the property, in terms of both size and location, as well as of the acquisitive power of its purchaser. The fact is that the members of the clergy in Valladolid had become a privileged class, both socially and economically. As a result, it had become common for them to reinvest

> *their income in memorial services, pious works and donations benefiting the church, in the form of chapels or figures, so as to suppress talk of the capital they invested in rural and urban properties.*[9]

9 Medina Rubio, *La Iglesia . . .*, p. 222.

Marín de Villaseñor died in 1664[10] and the house was inherited by Captain D. Manuel de Uribe y Severiche who was married to Doña Leonor de Contreras y Villaseñor Cervantes. In reality, it is here where the story of the house which survives today, the House of the Diezmo, begins. The new owner ordered the existing structure, whose adobe walls were in a deteriorated state, demolished and constructed a new, one-story house of quarry stone.[11] This simple structure was organized around a central courtyard delimited by Tuscan columns which supported semicircular arches whose extrados contained moldings, creating arcades along all four sides of this rectangular space.

10 Juárez Nieto, op. cit., p.139. Mazín, *El Cabildo . . .*, pp. 176-177. Bishop Fray Marcos Ramírez de Prado was obliged to intervene in the matter concerning the Steward of the Catedral, Marín de Villaseñor who, upon his death, owed the Catedral, in tithes and in rents administrated by the Church, a total of $41,441 pesos.

11 Ibid.

Houses of this type still exist in Morelia, in the República and Independencia neighborhoods. They are of one story, the interior spaces distributed around a central courtyard which features arcades along two, three or four of its sides. In most cases, there was also a secondary, service courtyard and sometimes a garden/orchard or a space for lodging animals.[12]

12 See: Ramírez Romero, *Morelia . . .*, p. 43.

The Age of Enlightenment

The diverse authors who have focused on this period in the history of Michoacán are in agreement that it was plagued by agricultural crises and epidemics throughout the eighteenth century, but little has been written

63
Baname

CAJA
CAJA
CAJA
7
CAJA
9 CAJA

about the construction activity. In fact, the period can be considered as something of an apex in such activity, examples including the Santuario de Guadalupe (1729-1736), the Church of the Capuchins (1737), the convent of Santa Catalina (1738), the façade and towers of the Cathedral (1740-1744), the Compañía (constructed toward the end of the 1740s), Las Rosas (1752), the Church of San Diego (1769), the Seminary (inaugurated on September 29, 1770) and San José (on which construction was begun in 1758 and which was inaugurated in 1776).[13] These works were complemented by others, in the second half of the century, such as the aqueduct and the Guadalupe causeway, which were encouraged by the clergy in Valladolid, headed by the prebendary José Pérez Calama, and which resulted in generating a great number of jobs.

So dynamic and enterprising was the clergy that they came to form an oligarchy of Spaniards and Creoles which possessed land and businesses. While the ownership of tracts of rural land continued to be a symbol of social prestige, commercial activity came to form one of the customs within this group. And although the Spanish aristocracy tended to think of commerce as a degrading activity, many Creoles turned to such undertakings, and with great success.

A specialization in the urban layout was consolidated, as well, in that status was measured by this society not only in terms of ethnicity and wealth but by the site which one occupied within the urban landscape. The best example of this was Real street in that between the Church of the Merced and the Church of the Monjas were to be found the houses of hacienda owners, the richest businessmen, the holders of the highest clerical positions and the secular authorities. Here lived the Spanish and the Creoles, the holders of power and wealth in Valladolid.[14]

Such was the case of the new owner of the house under study here, Don Simón de Espinosa y Monzón de la Huerta Agüero, who received it through an inheritance. He was a member of the council of Valladolid, a post he had also inherited in that it had previously been held by his grandfather, Francisco, and his father, Nicolás.[15] Espinosa y Monzón was married to Doña María de Campos Freire Torres Guerrero y Villaseñor Cervantes, a native of the town of Zamora and sister of the Venerable Madre Luisa de Santa Catalina, a member of the governing council of the Dominican convent in Valladolid, who died a virtual saint and whose life has been recorded by P. José Antonio Ponce de León.[16]

The new owner ordered the construction of a second story for the house and placed above the central balcony of the façade the coat of arms of the "Espinosas and Villaseñores." This type of addition became quite frequent in the eighteenth century, another example being the building which today houses the Museo Michoacán, a house which had belonged to Isidro de Huarte, a native of the Navarre region of Spain, who purchased it in 1772 and completed the addition of a second story in 1775.[17] A later example is the building, today known as the Casa de Morelos, which was constructed with one story in 1758. The house was acquired, in 1801, by José María Morelos who, in 1809, ordered the construction of a second story in which the mixtilinear Baroque style of the lower courtyard was repeated.[18]

13 Sigaut and Mazín, "El Cabildo . . . ," pp. 109-122.

14 Jaramillo, *La Vida . . .*, pp. 58-59.

15 Juárez Nieto, op. cit. p. 80. This is another interesting case of maintaining positions within a single family as well as the degree to which the practice of inheriting or purchasing public posts had spread. In 1661, Dr. D. Martín de Espinoza, prebendary of the Cathedral, ordered that the post of councilman, held by his brother José, would be passed on to his other brother, Nicolás.

16 Ibid.

17 Ibarrola Arriaga, op. cit., pp. 195-196. González Galván, *Arte Virreinal . . .*, n. p.

18 González Galván, op. cit., n. p.

Espinosa y Monzón was also the owner of the hacienda Uruétaro, in the Tarímbaro Valley and, like many hacienda owners, perhaps he had plans to enlarge the rear part of the house in order that he have storage space.

It is apparent that the repetition of the Tuscan order in the arcades along the north and south sides of the upper floor respond more to the forms already existing on the ground floor than to the styles in vogue at the time in that no paneled pilasters were employed. This modality was common in Valladolid after 1740, when José de Medina utilized paneled pilasters in the portals of the Cathedral.

The majority of houses of two stories, such as this one, were located along Real street (today Madero) and featured façades done in dressed quarry stone, the interior spaces distributed around a central courtyard, the service and storage areas distributed around a secondary courtyard, and a third courtyard for the drafts animals and the carriages. Houses such as these also required a large service staff. In the enormous canvas that captures the day the Dominican nuns of the convent of Santa Catalina de Siena moved to their new quarters on Real street, in 1738, a two-story house can bee seen, similar to the one we are discussing here, on whose balconies and roof can be observed numerous domestic servants, among them blacks, mulattos, mestizos and indigenous, watching the passing of the procession.[19] In the census records of the city of Valladolid from the eighteenth century, one can note that within each of these grand houses lived a veritable multitude, of great variety and diversity of race.

19 Sigaut, "Azucenas . . . ," pp. 199-215.

The chapel of the house was likely heavily adorned and its courtyard more beautiful that ever before when Doña Manuela, one of the daughters of the Espinosa y Monzón-Campos Freire marriage, was wed to a man from the Navarre region who her mother had carefully chosen for her. The groom, recently arrived in Valladolid, Don Antonio de Soravilla Azcárraga y Berrio, received as a dowry the sum of $20,000 pesos in Mexican silver. Upon her death, Doña Manuela's husband inherited the house as well as the hacienda Uruétaro.

This marriage produced four daughters: Micaela, María de los Dolores, María Ana and María Josefa. The second, María de los Dolores, entered into an unfortunate marriage with a man who squandered the fortune pertaining to her and her sisters and later fled Valladolid. From this marriage was born Juan de Dios Romero y Soravilla, who became the priest in Irimbo and took up arms when the war for independence began. His mother, María de los Dolores, was later imprisoned in Valladolid for providing supplies to the rebel troops.

Another of the Soravilla sisters had a son by a Knight of the Order of Alcántara, Don José Bernardo de Foncerrada y Ulibarri. He was born on February 24, 1782, in Valladolid, and was to become Captain Juan Nepomuceno de Foncerrada y Soravilla.

The grave economic situation of the Soravilla sisters led them, in 1795, to rent part of the house for the storage of the first carriages for hire available in Valladolid. There were two coupé-style coaches, that circulated only within the city, as well as two large coaches which were utilized for transportation between neighboring cities and towns. The owner of the carriages was Francisco de Cendejas y Sandoval, who also maintained twenty draft mules.[20]

20 Ibarrola Arriaga, op. cit., p. 128.

The small income this provided the sisters was insufficient for the maintenance of such a house, however, and in 1798 they decided to sell it to the Fábrica Espiritual de la Santa Iglesia Catedral, who christened it the House of the Diezmo.[21]

21 Ibid.

To Caesar That Which Is Caesar's

The *diezmo* (tithe) was not the only source of ecclesiastical revenue, but it was doubtless the principle income for the cathedrals of New Spain. They also received donations and were left properties in the wills of the faithful, as well as benefited from pious foundations whose capital was often of great amounts.

The tithe was no more and no less than one tenth of the production of the fruits of the earth, including cattle raising, and was obligatory. The Spanish, Creole and mestizo farmers as well as the clergy and the religious orders were required to pay, although the orders enjoyed many privileges. Although the indigenous peoples were legally exempt from tithes, in reality a portion of the tribute due to the king on their part was deducted.[22]

22 Juárez Nieto, op. cit., pp. 166-167.

In a bishopric as rich as that of Michoacán, the collections turned out to be quite important. In 1783, for example, the *ramo de gruesa* or *masa decimal*, which were the designations used by the royal legislation and the canonical legislation for the total of the tithes collected annually, reached "863,907 pesos, 7 reales [and] 6 granos."[23]

23 Mazín, "Presentación," p. 28.

There were two systems used to collect the part of the production corresponding to the tithe: through auction and administration. To this end, the territory of the bishopric was divided into nearly fifty sectors. The administrative judges and the auditor auctioned the tithed production to the highest bidder, who had to guarantee his bid with deposits, or administrators were named, usually a parish priest or another member of the clergy. However,

> *due to the frequency of the edicts that urged their punctual and complete fulfillment, it can be concluded that there was an ongoing tendency to avoid and commit fraud with regard to the payment of the tithes during the period of the viceroyalty, at least in Michoacán.*[24]

24 Ibid.

These problems surrounding the collection of the tithes are important, especially when one takes into account that in the bishopric of Michoacán, about 1770, there were ecclesiastical personnel assigned to these collections in 60% of the dioceses, particularly in the areas that had been, traditionally, the richest.

It is evident, however, that the policies of the Crown toward the clergy had been becoming tougher. Some of the measures serve to explain the circumstances which obliged the Cathedral of Valladolid to purchase a new tithe house, at a site so close to the Cathedral and "in a place so principal."

With the visit by José de Gálvez to Michoacán, in 1767, a strict tax had been placed on all cereal grains received by the public granaries. Just as the council of the Cathedral had placed demands on the cities through their administrators of the tithes, here they wanted to assert their immunity, but were unsuccessful. Additionally, in 1774, by a royal decree on October 19, the king now reserved the right to name the auditors of the tithes. This ended a long-standing tradition and inaugurated an unheard-of interference in the ecclesiastical administration.[25]

The creation of an intendancy in Valladolid, in 1787, also marked another step toward centralization and the establishment of a civil power that was capable of facing off with the ecclesiastical authorities. The fiscal pressure intensified. There was a steep increase in the costs of basic foods and products, and the city demanded greater and greater amounts of corn, leading to frequent shortages.[26]

Complex political and administrative maneuverings, both civil and ecclesiastical, are important to our understanding of why the building was acquired as the new House of the Tithe, in 1798. It is possible that the house had begun to function in the collection of the tithes that same year, according to entries in the book of accounts presented by the administrator of the tithes in Valladolid. In October of 1798 it was noted that corn had begun to be sold "at the new house of tithes." There were also entries regarding expenses for materials for the windows to protect against the entry of rainfall, and for the repair of an item where the corn was ground. Additionally, there was an entry noting an expenditure of 6 reals for materials to be used on the floors, to accommodate the corn "that began to be sold in said house on October 17."[27]

On various occasions the administrator of the tithes insisted in referring to the "new" house, which reinforces the certainty of the date of its acquisition. His accounts are of a noteworthy meticulousness, although this is not surprising if one considers that they had to pass the scrutiny of a jealous and alert city council. According to this same source, it appears that no major modifications were made to the house in that when such work was carried out on other tithe houses, such as those in Tarímbaro, Charo, Indaparapeo, Sinquio or Zinapécuaro, the accounts noted them with great clarity. With the same attention to detail, the amounts of what were received in corn, wheat, barley, flour, peppers, beans, peas, canary grass, cheese, sweets, fruit, chickens, calves, colts, mules, burros, goats, pigs, milk, wool and sheep were recorded, presenting the mosaic of the tithe system in Valladolid.

25 Mazín, "La Catedral . . . ," pp. 57 ff.

26 Mendoza Briones and Terán, "Repercusiones . . . ," vol. II, pp. 219-233.

27 "Cuentas de cargo y data que don Benito López, Administrador de los Diezmos de esta ciudad y sus anexos, presenta al Tribunal de Hacienda por los productos del año de 1798 y existencias de los que presentó del anterior de 97," Archivo Histórico Manuel Castañeda Ramírez, Fondo Cabildo, Sección Administración Pecuniaria, Serie Colecturía, Subserie Diezmos, f. 27v.

The Liberal Transformation

Without a doubt, the eighteenth century was marked by tense relations between Church and State. Before the independence movement, the tension had revolved around the tithes, and during said movement, the loyalty to the Spanish Crown on the part of the high clergy had created problems. In the case of Valladolid, Bishop-elect Manuel Abad y Queipo was moved to excommunicate the priest Miguel Hidalgo, leader of the insurgents, as well as his

companions. This extreme measure wasn't the only one taken by the clergy against the rebels in that

> *Abad y Queipo ordered the melting of the great bell in order to cast pieces of artillery and equipped a defense force under the command of the prebendary Don Agustín Ledos, to resist the attack of an army of nearly 60,000 insurgents.*[28]

28 Estrada de Gerlero, "El tesoro . . . ," p. 161.

During the two days that Hidalgo was in Valladolid, he took $400,000 pesos from the coffers of the cathedral, pertaining to the Church, as well as another $300,000 pesos which had been deposited there for safekeeping by private citizens. But this probably did not satiate Hidalgo in that due to the nearby location of the House of the Diezmo, with its storerooms replete with foodstuffs, it was certainly also looted by the rebel leader.

The problem of the tithes had become a thorn in the side of the relationship between the Mexican State, the Holy See and the local Church. All negotiations had been fruitless, and the forced credits the Church was obliged to provide, beginning just before the invasion by the United States, worsened the situation. The wealth of the Church versus the interests of the nation became a controversial issue, the government considering the clergy as a mere repository of these possessions while the Church felt that it was the rightful owner.

In spite of the political situation, Morelia (as Valladolid was now known), with its nearly 15,000 inhabitants, was termed by Madame Calderón de la Barca, on a visit in 1841, "a beautiful city,"

> *greatly admiring the wide and airy streets, the fine houses, the handsome public buildings, but especially the cathedral, the college and the churches.*[29]

29 Calderón de la Barca, op.cit., p. 503.

As to the house, there is nothing recorded until President Ignacio Comonfort issued the Ley de Desamortización de Bienes Civiles y Eclesiásticos (Law of Disentailment of Civil and Ecclesiastical Properties), on June 25, 1856. In Morelia, the law was announced by Dr. Miguel Silva on July 3, and went into effect on July 5. In the application of the law, certainly important was the administration of the governor, Epitacio Huerta (1858-1860), who confronted the conservative party as well as the stiff battle waged by the religious orders, particularly the Augustinians and by Bishop Clemente de Jesús Munguía, in defense of the ecclesiastical properties.

It appears, however, that the House of the Diezmo was "the first ecclesiastical building sold off by the authorities."[30] Although the sale was not legalized until 1862, the building was occupied in 1859, as borne out by records showing that the purchaser, a Prussian named Daniel Backhaussen, had been making monthly payments since December 7 of that year. The total price of the sale, negotiated between Backhaussen and the head of the state's finance department, Tranquilino

30 Sánchez, "Desamortización . . . ," vol. III, p. 48.

Valera, was $10,331.20 pesos, payable in bonds, of which the buyer presented $6,198.75 pesos, with the rest to be paid in monthly installments, of which he had already paid $2632.59, leaving a balance owing of $1449.91.[31]

31 *Archivo de Notarías de Morelia,* Escribano Nicolás Pérez, contrato de venta, 10 de marzo de 1862, f. 32v-34.

The contract specifies the considered measurements of the property, excluding the two stables which were located on each side of the house, a smaller one of 5.02 x 7.54 m, on the east side, and the larger, 5.02 x 10.90 m, on the west side, "noting that they are situated outside the area designated and their roofs pertain to the house belonging to the estate of Sr. Licenciado Benigno Ugarte," which bordered the north side of the house.[32]

32 *Archivo de Notarías de Morelia,* Escribano Ramón Huerta. Escritura Pública No. 137, 17 de octubre de 1896, fs. 220 and 220v.

Morelia was living through a difficult period, and the criticism directed toward the city's government, with regard to the maintenance of the city, was quite severe. One such complaint, written in 1870, paints a terrible picture of the city in which

> *the streets remain for entire weeks with great piles of garbage, the intersections seem like lakes, whose far from crystalline waters exhale insufferable miasmas; the street lighting is so poor that perhaps it would be better left to the pale brilliance of the stars; those bearing cargo or water use the sidewalks, blocking the way, and there have been occasions on which this abuse has caused grave injury to the pedestrians.*[33]

33 Tavera Alfaro, *Morelia . . . ,* vol. I, pp. 196-97.

It is unknown what work the new owner may have done on the house, but it is worth mentioning that the Europeans living in Morelia at the time spoke out frequently on the subject of the beauty of the city and the need to orient the improvements toward a rational, rather than luxurious, utilization of the few available resources. While the residents of Morelia looked on in silence, a Prussian named Othon Welda and a Belgian architect and builder, Baron Wodon de Sorinne, undertook the "beautification" of Paseo de San Pedro avenue between 1868 and 1869. Even without access to the historical data, it is possible to assume that while the house, now the Hotel de Michoacán, was the property of Backhaussen, many of the European ideas of "good taste," of the "civilized world" and of the "beautification" of public spaces were incorporated by him into a building of amiable appearance.

The Hotel de Michoacán

When Daniel Backhaussen died, the property was divided equally between his two children, Catarina and Félix Backhaussen, as recorded in a probate document from October 30, 1882. On October 17, 1896, the heirs sold the Hotel de Michoacán to a Frenchman, thirty-three years old and a bachelor, named Gustave Richaud. One of the children, Catarina Elvira Backhaussen de Félix, was living in Hamburg and the other, Félix, had died. His widow, Cora Balling de Grace, had remarried and was living in Mexico City. Finding the administration of the property from such great distances impossible, the two women had decided to sell it.

The sale of the Hotel de Michoacán is a good example of how credit operations functioned in Morelia during the period. The total price for the property, including the two aforementioned stables, was $16,000 pesos, of which Richaud paid $14,300 to Catarina Backhaussen, leaving a balance owing of $1,700 which he promised to pay in six years, at 6% annual interest and payable in bimonthly installments. But it was not to be that easy. Richaud had also received a loan from Audiffred Hermanos in the amount of $8,000 pesos. The term of this loan was also six years, at 9% annual interest and with the option of canceling half of the capital in three years. Under this arrangement, the property was mortgaged to Audiffred Hermanos, with Catarina Backhaussen holding secondary rights.[34]

> *As a counterpart to the limitation of the role carried out by the Church, in the decade of the 80s of the nineteenth century, a group of secular moneylenders was found to be fully consolidated within the state's economy, integrated mostly by important businessmen, hacienda owners and professionals, whose activities allowed them to accumulate considerable sums of money in cash which they began to employ in usurious loans, a business which turned out to be quite profitable.*[35]

The consequences for those who depended on this system of credit were, generally, fatal. Perhaps it was debt that obliged Richaud to sell the Hotel de Michoacán to Miguel Mesa, on July 9, 1900, as recorded in Public Deed No. 47, processed by the notary Ramón Huerta. The next transaction in the history of the building occurred on August 4, 1924, when Mesa sold the property, in three equal and indivisible parts, to his children María Esperanza, Eugenio and Humberto Mesa, although in 1927 he bought back the share pertaining to his son Eugenio. The hotel was mortgaged twice, in 1933 and 1934, and although it had changed owners, it had been rented, since 1906, to Germán Figaredo.

The Hotel Morelos

Two important governors impacted Michoacán in the 1920s and 1930s: Francisco J. Múgica (1920-1922) and Lázaro Cárdenas (1928-1932). Both administrations were marked by – as well products of – the process of centralization of the Mexican government. Historians see the period as a process consisting of the displacement of the regional oligarchies, pertaining to the long period corresponding to President Díaz' administration, by the new revolutionary

34 *Archivo de Notarías de Morelia*, Escribano Ramón Huerta. Escritura No. 137, 17 de octubre de 1896, fs. 219-232.

35 García Ávila, "El crédito . . . ," vol. III, p. 209.

groups, as well as the centralization of power in the executive branch of the federal government.

The process of the weakening of the regional oligarchies, of both of the types just mentioned, had distinct characteristics in the diverse regions of the country. In some areas, the old groups merged with the new ones while in other areas they were "swept away by the emergence of new groups and powerful regional leaders, giving way, in turn, to a new oligarchy."[36]

36 Zepeda Patterson, "Michoacán . . . ," vol. IV, p. 131.

In 1930, Morelia was a peaceful provincial capital that had just reached a population of 40,000 inhabitants, and Lázaro Cárdenas was an important member of the political leadership of the country, although of secondary stature. By the time he left his post as governor, in 1932, he formed part of the select group of politicians who governed Mexico. No one would have suspected, however, that within two years he would become the new president,

> *least of all his enemies, who took advantage of his departure by attacking him with great determination. This counteroffensive was fomented, in fact led, by Cárdenas' own successor, Gen. Benigno Serrato (1932-1934).*[37]

37 Ibid., p. 148.

This period of history, with regard to the house in question, ends with Lázaro Cárdenas' ascendancy to the presidency, in December of 1934, and the death of Gen. Serrato, in a plane crash, two days later. Less than a year after the his death, Serrato's widow, Abigail Reyes, bought the hotel.

The Hotel Morelos, as it was now called, was acquired by her on November 21, 1935, for the amount of $46,000 pesos.[38] She sold the two stables, mentioned in the foregoing as being on the east and west sides of the building, on November 3, 1956, to another widow, Eugenia Lance Viuda de Montes, for the sum of $14,800 pesos.[39]

38 *Registro Público de la Propiedad del Estado de Michoacán*, tomo 155, registro No. 29471 and Escritura Pública No. 971 del 15 de noviembre of the same year.

39 According to Comprobante 2002, of the Notario Público Licenciado Javier Ibarrola, cited in *Registro Público de la Propiedad del Estado de Michoacán*, tomo 705, registro No. 130749.

It is interesting to note that the hotel continued to be operated by the Figaredo family. Don Fernando Figaredo, the last manager, recalls that it had 42 rooms; that the staircase connecting the two levels was located at the entrance, just to the east; that in the secondary courtyard there were three bowling tables; that the bar, located on the east side, was one of the most popular in Morelia; that to one side of the bar was an area for billiards; and that the arcades along the east and west sides of the upper floor had been closed off, creating six rooms on each side. The volume on the north side of the upper floor housed the laundry and ironing facilities. Finally, he remembers being invited to tour the building with its new owners and was present when the building was inaugurated as a branch of Banco Nacional de México.

Banco Nacional de México

This bank has a long history in Morelia. In reality, the activities of Banco Nacional de México began in the city in 1902, together with those of Banco del Estado de México. They were responding to the new political-economic model, marked by the accumulation of mercantile capital, the growth in foreign trade, the modernization and expansion in mining, and the opening of the railways, facts which, when taken together, accentuated the need for banking institutions.

The banks put into circulation great amounts of money yet did not manage to resolve the needs for the capital necessary to increase production in the agricultural sector. Their impact on the overall regional economy, however, was very important, especially on the part of Banco Nacional de México "which was initiated with the most considerable of the [capitalizations] that was registered in those years: $20,000,000 pesos."[40]

Inmuebles Banamex, the bank's real estate arm, purchased the Hotel Morelos from Abigail Reyes on April 11, 1967, for the quantity of $1,050,000 pesos.[41] The surface area covered by the building totals 1594.18 m^2. The outside dimensions are irregular due to the earlier sale of the two stables along the sides of the building. As such, it measures 26.25 m across the front and 27.30 m at the back. The east side is divided into three planes, one of 45.70 m, south to north, at which point the wall juts out 60 cm and then continues northward another 14.60 m^2 adjacent to the Teatro Mexicano, formerly the Cine Eréndira movie house. The west side measures 60.30 m, adjacent to the Bancomer bank building which was once the house of the head of the city government of Valladolid, Don Gabriel García de Obeso, built in 1783.

Banco Nacional de México made modifications to the building in order to adapt it for its new uses. To the east of the entrance, where the staircase had been located, were placed the automated teller machines. To the west of the entrance is an elevator in part of what once had been one of the rooms of the house. The arcades along both sides of the central courtyard were given over to office areas. Those on the upper floor were closed off, forming hallways along the east and west sides, respecting the Tuscan order of the columns and the valances that are repeated beneath each gargoyle. The rooms that overlook the street on the second level, which were certainly the most important rooms in the original house, are occupied by the executive offices. The entire north wing, occupied by offices, features a wall formed by four arches, now filled in which, in their day, were open and looked onto the secondary courtyard. Both courtyards have been roofed, in a rather unfortunate manner.

The façade is sober and possesses few decorative elements. There are smooth jambs, small cornices, a lintel which signals the entrance to the house and a bare, oval medallion which, throughout the history of the house, was surely occupied by distinct motifs: the proud coats of arms of proud families or an ecclesiastical insignia when the house was used to collect the tithes in old Valladolid.

In contrast to other nearby buildings, whose façades were greatly modified in accordance with the eclectic currents, this house conserves a precision in which can be appreciated an elegant combination of material and technique.

40 García Ávila, op. cit., p. 222.

41 *Registro Público de la Propiedad del Estado de Michoacán*, tomo 705, registro No. 130749, f. 300.

The finely cut quarry-stone ashlars, meant to be exposed and not plastered over, reflect the intense sunlight from the unpolluted skies of Morelia.

The common phrases heard here are charged with an ancient, popular wisdom if we understand them in the sense of being connected, apart from the universe of knowledge, also to the fears, the taboos, the prohibitions, the myths and the fantasies of the inhabitants who lived here throughout the course of the area's history. One of these common phrases is that which says that "*one doesn't want what one doesn't know.*" The objective of these pages has been to create a connection, a personal and emotional bridge to this house, an example of the country's patrimony. Its protection, conservation and care may be aided if I have succeeded.

The House of the Count del Valle de Súchil

Durango, Durango

The House of the Count del Valle de Súchil

The house of the Count del Valle de Súchil, in Durango, is doubtless the most beautiful example of civil architecture from the era of the viceroyalty, not only in this city but in all of northern Mexico. Certainly no other mansion constructed in this period within said region can rival it. A product of the urban development that characterized this city in the eighteenth century, the capital of Nueva Vizcaya, a province of the vast viceroyalty of New Spain, it also represented the social status of its first owner. Joseph Ignacio del Campo Soberón y Larrea, Count del Valle de Súchil, was a man whose career can be considered paradigmatic of the rise and enrichment dreamed of by all of the colonists, although reached by very few of them.

Clara Bargellini

The building is situated on the southwest corner of the intersection of what are today Cinco de Febrero and Francisco Madero streets, formerly Real and San Francisco streets. At that very corner, on a faceted wall, is the principal entrance to the house. In order to better understand the positioning of the Count's house, one must be aware that, originally, the entrance faced a small plaza surrounded by a complex of Franciscan buildings which included the Church of San Francisco, the convent of San Antonio and the Chapel de la Tercera Orden. The entrance to the house formed one of the façades that surrounded this octagonal intersection-plaza. Unfortunately, the Franciscan structures were barbarously demolished in 1917, resulting not only in the loss of buildings of great importance to the history and identity of Durango but, also, the destruction of the surroundings which had given full meaning to the peculiar solution of placing the entrance to the house at the corner, as well as the justification for the stark contrast between rich detail of the entrance façade and the sobriety of the two other faces of the building which define its rectangular dimensions.

It is interesting to note that the side of the house that faces Cinco de Febrero presents a symmetrical arrangement in the fenestration as well as a certain amount of ornamentation.[1] This wall forms a distinct façade which fronts what once was the city's principal avenue. The frames of the windows rise to the cornice and then onward to frame the windows of the second floor. As such, they create continuous vertical accents, from top to bottom, that serve as a counterpart to the grand, horizontal cornice that wraps around the entire building and signals the basic division between the two floors. The combination of elements provides a visual balance. The façade facing Francisco Madero no longer conserves its original fenestration.

In the design of the entrance, there is an evident desire to frame the various details with strong elements, such as the pilasters of quarry-stone ashlars whose upper cornice is topped by two large pinnacles. It is also clear that the richness of ornamentation was meant to be concentrated on the upper level. As such, the door on the ground floor is framed by rectilinear pilasters while above are *estípite* (a style that recalls a truncated, inverted pyramid) pilasters and panels covered with relief work. Of course, the ground floor features its own ornamentation, introducing motifs that are repeated throughout the building. There are reliefs with Rococo motifs on the pilasters and the frieze, including *rocaille* motifs, shells, wreaths, ribbons, fruit and flowers, all placed according to a strict symmetry. The lintel of the entrance is slightly elevated and the pendant of the keystone is eye-catching. The relief work that decorates it is of an uneven style that suggests a later intervention. Outstanding is a large diamond at the center, of fine craftsmanship, which bears the monogram "MD," indicating that these elements are from the nineteenth century, when the house was the property of Maximilian Damm. The frieze and the panels with dense relief work, as well as the central pilasters of this first level, with their zigzag striation on the lower third, are the first taste of what is to be found in the principal courtyard.

The upper floor is also dominated by a doorway which, in this case, opens onto a balcony surrounded by a splendid railing executed in forged iron. At the center of the mixtilinear door frame there is another version of the pendant keystone. Here, we find a slight depression in the molding, as if to receive the base of the pedestal which corresponds, in turn, to a niche above the door. The vaulted niche houses an image, in quarry stone, of San José (Joseph), the patron saint of the original owner of the house, with the Christ Child in his arms. Around the niche is more Rococo ornamentation, in relief. Above is the cornice where, at each end, pinnacles top the axes of the supports of the two volumes of the entrance. The cornice opens at the center, coiling itself into volutes so as, seemingly, to allow the ascendance of the niche. The technique of the carving in the helmet at the upper part identifies it as part of the renovations carried out in the nineteenth century.

From the principal entrance, one passes through a vestibule and on to the first courtyard. Immediately, attention is drawn to the arch, with its pendant keystone, in the arcade opposite the entrance. It is by now evident that this motif was preferred by the building's architect as attractive and worthy of the extraordinary courtyard that it introduces. The courtyard is surrounded on all four sides by arcades formed by arches and columns covered with zigzag reliefs.

1 Although the fenestration is original, it had to be reconstructed during the most recent restoration work on the house. This work was based on a photograph from 1870. I am indebted, for this information as well as all the other data included herein regarding the changes the building has suffered, to the kindness of architect Luis Sergio Rivera Damm who himself undertook much of the recent restoration work. I am grateful to Rivera Damm for his generosity in sharing his broad knowledge of the building as well as the remembrances of his forebears.

This geometric motif begins at the bases of the columns, where it is arranged horizontally, then follows the vertical column shafts and continues on to the depressed arches that unite the columns. Foliage fills the spandrels, and a frieze with diamond and oval shapes completes the articulation of the ground floor. On the second floor, there is less ornamentation. The columns are fluted but sober, and there is simple railing with caryatids with baskets on their heads at the center of each section, seemingly to protect the passersby. The spandrels are filled with foliage and Rococo details. A basket motif stands out at the center of the east side on the upper floor. The ensemble is topped by an undulating cornice that features sharp points that correspond to the axes of the columns. This motif, as with so many others in the house, appeared here for the first time in the civil architecture of Durango.

In the arcade on the southern side of the courtyard, another arch with a pendant keystone marks the foot of the staircase. On the side of the arch visible from the staircase, the keystone is sculpted with a grotesque with garlands of flowers that emerge from its mouth. At the point of the keystone hangs a pomegranate. Above it can be appreciated a basket with foliage and flowers. The staircase is comprised of two flights, illuminated by a an opening in the wall which looks onto the other courtyard. From the landing, a third flight descends to the east, terminating in an area from which there is access, through a side door, to Francisco Madero street and to the secondary courtyard. This flight is the result of an intervention in the twentieth century since, originally, the staircase simply rose to the second floor from the principal courtyard, as was usual in this type of structure.

It is important, here, to take another look at the carved quarry stone that so characterizes this building, to note some of the features and to register the different motifs that are to be found scattered throughout the principal courtyard. Not all of the stone carving is of the same quality and excellence, which might be expected in a house of this enormity. Surely there were a number of master stonecutters who participated in the work. The striated columns of the ground floor, with their geometric ornamentation, present a robust and strong appearance that contrasts with the delicate relief work of leaves, fruit and flowers, especially that of the spandrels on the upper floor and the frames of some of the interior doors. Particularly notable is the entrance to the grand drawing room on the second floor. There are also more indications of restorations and changes in some of the detailing, such as the case of the keystone of the building's principal entrance, as mentioned earlier. Another important example is to be found, while descending the stairs, at the center of the arch with its pendant keystone. Here, the technique in the carving of the foliage, of deep, precise cuts, and other motifs such as roses, are from the nineteenth century. It can be assumed that, here, the relief work was altered, either because it was no longer appreciated by later owners or because it had been damaged and required repair. During recent restoration work, some of the pieces and stone carvings were renovated, copying the originals that still exist.

The original ornamentation is typical of the period of the construction of the house, and a number of the motifs have already been mentioned. Included in the relief work of the spandrels, pilasters, frames and door panels are cornucopias, baskets, mermaids, grotesques, flowers, fruit, caryatids and small faces, some at the center of medallions. These elements are surrounded and connected by shells, *rocaille*, leaves, garlands, bows, ribbons and draperies. All of the foregoing are motifs that suggest abundance and gaiety, quite appropriate to such a majestic house. There are also valances on the bases of the columns. Of great importance are the fragments of the original mural painting. The largest of these is on the wall along the staircase that connects the two courtyards. Originally, it was within a rectangular room which was reduced in size in order to make way for this additional flight. It contains motifs painted with foliage, similar to that of the relief work, in dark blue against a white background. Currently, the house is painted as it was in the period known as the Porfiriato (1876-1911), but some examples from the eighteenth century remain as well. Quite noteworthy are the original doors, carved in a combination of various types of wood and containing many of the motifs already mentioned. Finally, many of the original beams have been conserved, as well as their corresponding planks.

As with the principal courtyard, the service courtyard is of two stories. It has arcades on only three of its sides, however, and is decorated more simply. Instead of striated columns there are smooth pillars, devoid of any relief work. Originally, to reach the upper level, there was a wooden staircase in one of the corners at the rear. The fountain is a later addition, neither this nor the principal courtyard having had one. The fountain appearing in archival photographs is not from the period of the viceroyalty but from the nineteenth century, an addition made by the Damm family.

We turn now to a closer examination of the distribution and identification of the spaces within the house. As has been noted, everything is organized around the two courtyards, the principal and the secondary, or service, courtyard, and the flight of stairs that connects the two is not original, such that, prior to this intervention, the division between the two was more distinctly marked. Of course, originally, neither of the two courtyards was roofed, as the principal of the two is today. The spaces around the grand courtyard were of greater size though, unfortunately, few of the original interior walls remain today. It is probable that to the left of the entrance, along what was then San Francisco street, there were offices and spaces dedicated to commerce. To the right of the vestibule is a broad space, interrupted only by columns. It must be noted, however, that the second row of columns is new, copied from the originals. They were added in the twentieth century when the walls of the two rooms on this side were eliminated in order to create a large space required by the El Gran Número Once warehouse. Outstanding is the large drawing room on the upper floor, a space typical of this kind of building, which was the site of the more ceremonial functions within the house. Of note are the three balconies accessible from this room which look out onto what was Real street.[2] Here were hung fabrics and tapestries on holidays while the family and

2 The architect Rivera Damm considers that these balconies are not from the era of the viceroyalty but, rather, from the nineteenth century, and that the originals might have been of wood.

8 CAJA
11 CAJA

guests observed the processions in the street. The roof is noteworthy and, in the main, original.[3]

3 The installation of a metal ceiling panel, by Maximilian Damm, in the nineteenth century, had mutilated the columns' capitals. It was possible to reconstruct them, however, because two complete columns survived, within a wall that had been added, and were used as a model in the restoration work.

A still unanswered question is whether or not the house contained a private chapel since none of the existing spaces provide evidence of having served this function. Perhaps among the carved stone there was an inscription or a cross that identified the location but, today, there are no explicitly religious symbols in any part of the building. If one did exist at some point, it was eliminated by one of the owners in the nineteenth century. On the second floor, however, in the area surrounding the service courtyard, there is a small, attractive space with a small cupola that might have, at one time, been an oratory. Curious, however, is its location in an area of the house of lesser hierarchy, as well as its small size. One must conclude, for the present, that the lack of evidence indicates that the house did not include a chapel.

Throughout this description, reference has been made to elements which suggest that the house of the Count del Valle de Súchil was constructed just after the midpoint of the eighteenth century. The *estípite* pilasters at the entrance, the parallel presence of pilasters and columns of a sobriety rooted in the Classical style, and the decorative vocabulary of the Rococo all point to this period. Effectively, the scant, specific information that exists on the house confirm this dating. The first mention comes in a document pertaining to the Cathedral of Durango, dated May 20, 1763, which notes that the completion of the side entrance portals of the main church had been commissioned to the "master builder" that had been "involved in the work for Don Joseph Larrea," the future Count del Valle de Súchil.[4] This master was Pedro de Huertas, and he was contracted for the completion of said entrances on January 30, 1764.[5] It is quite possible, therefore, that the house had been completed prior to the date when the architect moved on to undertake the work on the church. Clearly, the Count's house was finished by September-October of 1777 since, at this time, it served to lodge the nobleman Teodoro de Croix and his retinue, which included a priest, Juan Agustín de Morfi, who recorded the fact.[6] The census of Durango of 1778 notes the identity of the owner. Registered is

4 Archivo de la Catedral de Durango, Libro VII, ff. 13v-14. This document refers to Joseph del Campo Soberón y Larrea by his final surname, which is how he normally signed his name.
Gallegos, *Historia . . .* , p. 423. Here can be found a copy of Larrea's signature.

5 Archivo de la Catedral de Durango, op. cit., f. 37v.

6 Morfi, *Diario y derrotero . . .* , p. 82.

> *a main house of two stories, all in ashlar stonemasonry, balconies and windows of iron, property of the Count del Valle de Súchil, Don Joseph del Campo y Larrea, who lives at his hacienda at Muleros, and today this said house is under the care of Don Benito Rosales, official of the Real Caja in this city.*[7]

7 Saravia, "Padrón . . . ," vol. IV, p. 265.

As few as they may be, these documents provide the name of the architect of the house, the information that the work had been initiated by the middle of 1763 and that it had been finished prior to 1777, perhaps more than a decade before this date, in 1764. Additionally, all of the characteristics of the construction pointed out in the foregoing indicate that the architect had knowledge of this

type of residence and was experienced in his art. The solution he chose for the principal, corner entrance, as well as the arches with their large, pendant keystones, for example, were employed for the first time in New Spain by the architect Pedro de Arrieta, at the beginning of the 1730s, in the Palacio de la Inquisition in Mexico City.[8]

At any rate, the history of a building neither begins nor ends with the dates of its construction or the names of its owner and architect. That such a magnificent house should come to be constructed in Durango is the sum total of a number of factors relative to the urban and architectural development of the city as well as the fortunes of the man who commissioned it and the one who built it.

In the eighteenth century, Durango was a growing city. Founded in 1563 with thirteen heads of households and their families,[9] its development had not been easy. Only at the beginning had the growth in population been steady. Bishop Mota y Escobar, on a visit in 1605, noted that "its location is marvelous, on some clear, flat land next to some abundant hot springs, the water from which passes through trenches along all of the streets in the town." There were now fifty households of Spaniards, in houses "all of adobe of one story, of moderate structure and capacity."[10] In 1620, the households numbered 150 and a bishopric was established, but the war with the indigenous Tepehuan people (1616-18) and the discovery of the mines at San José Parral, in 1631, caused a prolonged decline in Durango's fortunes as a city. By 1663, the population had dropped to the point where the bishop had asked for the elimination of the diocese.[11] The governor had long ago moved to Parral. In 1681, only forty heads of households were registered as living in the capital of Nueva Vizcaya.

The city's recovery dates to the early years of the eighteenth century. Little by little the population began to increase and the buildings began to be improved. In the census of 1707, there were eighty-four Spanish heads of households and another 103 non-Spanish. One source mentions 700 heads of households in 1716. About this time, the reconstruction of the cathedral was well under way.[12] About 1714, the city government had also decided to reconstruct the town hall and related buildings, a granary and a jail.[13] Closer to the dates that concern the house, Bishop Pedro Tamarón y Romeral wrote, in 1765: "Each day this city is experiencing new growth; in terms of its buildings; large houses are being constructed with ample comforts and beautiful gardens."[14] He might well have been referring to the house of the Count del Valle de Súchil.

In fact, a few years earlier, in 1759, Joseph Ignacio del Campo Soberón y Larrea had inherited an enormous fortune from his father-in-law. It is known, regarding the title he was granted by Charles III, that Larrea was "a native of the Consejo de San Pedro de Galdamez in the Señorío de Vizcaya."[15] The document continues:

Since your early years, imitating your forebears, having come to America and the Kingdom of Nueva Vizcaya, you dedicated yourself to royal service in the Real y Minas at Santiago de Mapimí, one of the

8 Maza, *El arte colonial . . .*, pp. 21-22. The author also notes that a similar, faceted entrance façade had been employed, in 1764, in the Casa de Moneda, in San Luis Potosí. He considers that this house predates that of the Count del Valle de Súchil. At the time of his writing, however, the documents cited earlier indicate that Huertas executed his work prior to that of the house in San Luis Potosí.

9 Gerhard, *The North . . .*, p. 204. Unless otherwise noted, all subsequent references to population are taken from this work.

10 Mota y Escobar, *Descripción geográfica . . .*, p. 83. Again the population is registered in terms of the number of heads of households, making the overall population much greater.

11 Porras Muñóz, *Iglesia y estado . . .*, pp. 203-204.

12 Bargellini, *La arquitectura . . .*, pp. 173-175.

13 Saravia, *Apuntes . . .*, vol. I, p. 329.

14 Tamarón y Romeral, *Demostración . . .*, p. 35.

15 Gallegos, op. cit., pp. 424-426. Unless otherwise noted, all the information on the life of Larrea has been culled from this work. Thanks to the kindness of friends in Durango, I have been able to examine the original, from which the subsequent quotations have been taken.

frontiers of those kingdoms, exposing your person in various campaigns in the extermination of the nation of Cocoyome Indians, distinguishing yourself among all the others present, not only in the performance with weapons, fervor and activity but, also, in aid at your cost to various individuals and to the servants and dependents that you have in the Real y Minas with provisions, arms and munitions.

The text seems to indicate that Joseph Ignacio arrived in New Spain when he was a child or that he had relatives already living there, a frequent situation among the colonists. The date of his arrival might be fixed as being around 1750 when considering all of the other data available relative to his life. The mention of hostilities between the colonists and the indigenous tribe in the frontier area of Bolsón de Mapimí suggests that he participated in the strengthening of the garrisons in that area.[16]

Fundamental to Larrea's fortune was his marriage, in 1752, to Isabel Erauzo, a rich Creole woman.[17] In doing so, he was repeating the history of his father-in-law as well as of many other Spaniards who accumulated fortunes during this period.[18] Isabel's ancestors included, on her mother's side, Pedro de Hermosillo, a native of Sanlúcar de Barrameda, in Andalusia, Spain, who had lived at the San Martín mines, near Sombrete, and who was one of the soldiers who had accompanied Francisco de Ibarra in his conquest of the north.[19] One of Hermosillo's descendants, Josefa Francisca de Inunigarro, married Manuel Ruiz de Somocurso, who became rich from the mines at Texamen. Esteban de Erauzo, Isabel's father, a native of Villabona, Guipúzcoa, in Spain, married the daughter of Manuel Ruiz in 1732. He eventually received the mines pertaining to his father-in-law and continued to exploit them. He also controlled the mines at San José de Avino and had an interest in the mines at Nuestra Señora de Aránzazu de Gamón, all of which led to his becoming one of the richest men in the province. Because Esteban de Erauzo and his wife, Leogarda Ruiz de Somocurso, had only two children, Pedro and Isabel, and because Pedro had followed an ecclesiastical path, upon Esteban's death, in 1759, the management of his businesses was passed on to his son-in-law, Joseph Ignacio del Campo y Larrea.

Del Campo y Larrea strengthened his financial and social power with political power. Upon his arrival in Nueva Vizcaya, in April of 1761,[20] the new governor, Don Joseph Carlos de Agüero, decided to establish his residence in Durango.[21] His decision is decisive proof of the importance that the capital again possessed in that the preceding governors, for decades, had chosen to live in either Parral or Chihuahua, where the wealth of the province was concentrated. Agüero came to hold Larrea in high esteem, as witnessed in a document written by Charles III:

> *These services, your talent and disposition, recognized by the Governor of that kingdom . . . , you earned your being named Lt. Governor and Captain General of this same kingdom, with the*

16 Velázquez, "Los reglamentos" and "Los indios . . . ."

17 *Libro de casamientos de Pánuco 1743-1766*, Archivo Parroquial de San Juan del Río. Here the marriage is recorded, having taken place in San José de Avino on August 15, 1752.

18 Berrojalbiz and Miguel Vallebueno, "Grupos vascos . . . ," vol. I, pp. 246-263. With thanks to Miguel Vallebueno for his kindness and assistance.

19 Gallegos, op. cit., pp. 24-27. Here he notes information on Hermosillo found in *Información de méritos de Francisco de Ibarra*, conserved in the Archivo General de Indias.

20 Porras Muñóz, op. cit., pp. 94-95.

21 Ibid., p. 159.

approval of my Viceroy in New Spain and of the Audiencia de Guadalajara; and whose duties you undertook with individuality and the greatest acceptance during the absence of nineteen months by that Governor (in the protection and defense of the Castillo de San Juan de Ulúa, in the city and port of Veracruz).[22]

22 *Diligencias de cobranza contra el conde de Súchil de los derechos de media anata durante su interinato como gobernador*, Archivo Histórico del Gobierno del Estado de Durango, exp. 63, cajón 14.

At this point it is necessary to clarify something. Given the close relationship between Larrea and Governor Agüero, some believe that the house in Durango had originally been destined for occupation by Agüero. To date, not one document has been found to support this hypothesis. On the contrary, a number of documents from Agüero's administration point to problems surrounding his lodgings in Durango which prove, with sufficient certainty, that the governor had nothing to due, directly, with the luxurious residence of Larrea.[23] Prior to Agüero's arrival, in 1761, the city's secular officials had rented a house which was to be the residence of the governor during visits to city. Agüero insisted that the rent continue to be paid when he decided to reside permanently in Durango. The city officials protested that they shouldn't be required to cover such an expense, especially since the governor was now asking for a larger house than the one which had originally been utilized. Called on for a ruling, the attorney for the Audiencia de Guadalajara judged that the governor was within his rights and, on July 28, 1763, the court decided that the city had to contribute $250 pesos, annually, for such rent. It should be noted that this litigation was occurring at the same time as Larrea's house was under construction, as noted in the document to be found in the cathedral. As late as 1769 there are records noting the rental of a house for the governor, one which pertained to the dean of the cathedral, Don Salvador Becerra López de Osuna y Zárate, located across from the Church of San Agustín and which no longer exists.[24]

23 Porras Muñóz, op. cit., p. 160. Including the data that follows in this paragraph.

24 Saravia, "Padrón . . . ," op. cit., vol IV, p. 277. Noted here is "a large main house of two stories, frames, arcades and stairs of stonemasonry."

Larrea probably decided on the construction of his house after 1759, when he inherited the fortune from his father-in-law. The fact that his brother-in-law Pedro's house, "adobe, of one story, frames of stone with its small orchard of fruit trees," was located on the same block[25] suggests that the property was also part of his inheritance. Prior to this, Durango had not seen houses of two stories, as noted by Nicolás Lafora, in 1766.[26] As late as the census of 1778 there are few houses noted as having two stories. Additionally, Larrea's house was of stone and mortar, not adobe, something quite exceptional in Durango at the time. Although the possibility that Larrea had considered the advantage of having a house worthy of a tenant such as the governor cannot be completely ruled out, one must conclude that his principal motivation was that of enhancing his own image and of satisfying his yearnings for greatness.

25 Ibid., p. 265.

26 Lafora, *Relación . . .*, pp. 55-56. He states here that all of the houses were of one story.

His ambitions and his means were truly staggering. Rural property in the period of the viceroyalty was, apart from a source of income and collateral for credit, a status symbol. In 1771, Larrea acquired, from Joseph Gregorio

Robles, the enormous estate that comprised nearly all of the valleys of Poanas and Súchil, a principal source of wheat for the Real de Sombrete. This vast tract included the haciendas San Antonio de Muleros (today Vicente Guerrero), San Amador del Mortero, San Gregorio Magno, Guadalupe del Salto (el Saltito), Ojos de Santa Ana, Tapil, La Rabia, San Quintín, Goleta, Gomara, Tenaxa, Chachacuastle, Cieneguilla, San Pedro Mártir, Concepción, San Juan Bautista, San Diego de los Corrales, San Diego Mancha and San Miguel de la Laborcita.[27]

27 Parra, *San Diego . . .*, pp. 42-43.

With his mineral riches, his palatial house in the city and owning a great part of what is today the southern part of the state of Durango, Larrea sought that which he still lacked: a title from the Crown. This he received through a decree by Charles III on April 1, 1775. In achieving this, his friendship with Governor Agüero had served him well, as can be deduced from the text of the decree, as well as had a series of merits that were also listed in the document. Within the text it was noted that Larrea had

established a new town with fifty Spanish families, naming it Nuevo Bilbao y Nuestra Señora de Begoña, with the idea that it serve as a shield against the enemy nations that lie on the frontier, the town also having been supported at your expense in the year 1769 which was very calamitous; that you have inspected the mines at Avino, undertaking considerable and very costly work, to facilitate the removal of the metals and to process them at the populous hacienda you own on which you maintain more that two thousand laborers; that you have contributed to my royal treasury more than $200,000 pesos [in taxes], and more than $80,000 which in five years you have consumed in quicksilver, without including the amount of the rights to the great portions of silver foil, that you have paid the loans and provisions of so many workers fostering the towns and haciendas in the area, employing many in the labor at the mines and consuming from them with respect the fruit that they gather and the cattle that they raise; that so many advances your industrious fatigue has achieved resulting in the best service to me and increasing my Royal Finances, as has been recognized by the royal officials in Durango, admiring the great works you have done and continue to do and the difficulties that you have overcome exhibiting growing quantities at no profit.

The king continued by stating that "in view of all of this and for finding yourself with abundant properties and income with which to maintain with dignity and splendor any favor that I deign to bestow upon you, we concede you the Title of Castile for your person, your children, heirs and successors in perpetuity." The document was signed in Aranjuez on June 11, 1776. Although a short time later, on a visit to the aforementioned town of Nueva Bilbao, at the point where the Nazas River empties into the Laguna de Mayrán,[28] the nobleman Teodoro de Croix found nothing more than a corral and a few small trees, the very convincing wealth and his other merits had won Larrea the titles of

28 Morfi, op. cit., p. 58.

Viscount de San Juan de las Bocas and Count del Valle de Súchil.[29] Legend has it, in the town of Vicente Guerrero (formerly the Hacienda Muleros), that Charles III also gave the Count an olive tree, sent from Spain in a barrel, which still exists in the atrium of the town's church.

In 1774,[30] while still arranging for his title, Larrea selected, among his properties in the Súchil Valley, the hacienda San Amador del Mortero[31] as the site on which he was to build a beautiful house that included a chapel, and in whose construction can be observed many of the elements from the house in Durango. For example, the lintels of the principal portal, as well as the one opening onto the balcony, feature prominent keystones. There are valances and other decorative elements above the entrance that are similar to those of the house in the city.[32] Additionally, the sculpture of the patron saint is located in a niche framed by *estípite* pilasters on the façade of the chapel, and the profiles of the cornices, both of the house and the chapel, are characterized by an undulating movement. The rooms at the hacienda are organized around an enormous, full-height courtyard. In creating a staircase of five flights in a construction that is not vaulted, a pillar at the center of the foot of the first flight serves to support the upper floor. This is an original solution and causes one to believe that Pedro de Huertas had come to work again for his former patron. According to the census of 1778, cited earlier, the Count resided on the hacienda more than in the city.[33] Now, with this country mansion, we can guess that the Count del Valle de Súchil had achieved everything that he had sought. Upon his death, in 1782,[34] Joseph Ignacio del Campo Soberón y Larrea was the owner of mines, haciendas and two splendid houses, one in Durango and the other on the hacienda Mortero, between Muleros and the town of Súchil.

Little information exists on the architect Pedro de Huertas. However, the great quality of his work and his role in introducing the *estípite* as well as an incipient Neoclassical style to the architecture of Durango has assured his fame. His activity in the capital of Nueva Vizcaya followed that of the famous Felipe de Ureña who had been called to Durango in 1749 to create the main altar for the cathedral, which was dedicated ten years later.[35] In this work, unfortunately lost in the nineteenth century, except for a few fragments, the residents of Durango received their first introduction to the "modern" style, from Mexico City, which incorporated the *estípite*. With Huertas' work, they saw the *estípite* incorporated into a new ornamental vocabulary and applied to architecture. The ground floor of the Count's house, with its corner entrance, was also a novelty and probably served as a model for the Urquidi house in the Valley of San Bartolomé,[36] as well as, perhaps, others.

It is possible that Huertas had come to Durango on the behest of Joseph del Campo y Larrea. Miguel Vallebueno has uncovered documentation that identifies him as a mulatto and a native of Mexico City.[37] He was, perhaps, not a titled architect in that in no document is he referred to as such. Rather, he is referred to as an *alarife* (master builder or mason), and it is obvious that he knew stone carving because the figures he created for the side entrances to the cathedral

29 According to the document, the title of viscount was a prerequisite in obtaining the title of count, such that it was granted and, simultaneously, eliminated with the granting of the title Count del Valle de Súchil.

30 Vallebueno, *Haciendas* . . . , pp. 75-81. It is noted here that permission for the construction of a chapel on the hacienda was granted on November 25, 1774.

31 Gómiz, *Monografía* . . . , p. 52. The hacienda was so named by Vicente de Zaldívar, one of the earlier owners, who used it for processing minerals from the nearby Vacas mines. I am grateful to the De la Parra family for the opportunity to visit El Mortero.

32 A new coat of arms has been placed above the entrance, at the center, where Larrea's coat of arms had surely been located earlier. Curiously, there is no drawing of his coat of arms in the document granting him his title and, as such, it has been impossible to determine what it looked like.

33 The census states that the hacienda where he lived was Muleros, because it was the hacienda most important, economically, but the residence of the Count was on Mortero, which is very near.

34 Ladd, *La nobleza* . . . , p. 317. To date, no portrait of the Count is known to exist.

35 Bargellini, op. cit., pp. 178-179.

36 Bargellini, et al., *Historia y arte* . . . , p. 118.

37 Miguel Vallebueno, personal communication. Vallebueno plans to publish these documents.

were registered in documents as having been his. His architectural knowledge, however, clearly demonstrated in the house of the Count del Valle de Súchil, causes one to believe that he was surely more than a "master builder." Another point worthy of consideration is that if Larrea did indeed bring him to Durango for the project, his pride could hardly have been satisfied by a master who was anything less than a true architect.

Whatever the case may have been, surely there was no other architect or master builder in Durango at the time with the knowledge possessed by Pedro de Huertas. Bishop Pedro Tamarón y Romeral took advantage of his presence in the city in order to commission the completion of the cathedral. In 1764, he was charged with some repairs[38] and, in 1765, he finished the secondary volumes of both of the side entrances[39] whose forms are very similar to those of the Count's house, as observed many years ago, with his accustomed sagacity, by Francisco de la Maza.[40] Pedro de Huertas seems to have remained working at the cathedral in that church documents record his name as late as March of 1769 as having carried out other, small-scale construction work.[41] In addition, he was surely charged with enlarging the window and elevating the height of the principal entrance to the cathedral, as can be seen in the ornamentation which surrounds these two elements.[42] There is one more work in Durango that is possibly his, a one-story house with a beautiful entrance portal with a door whose lintel features a pendant keystone and an undulating frame which recalls the magnificent entrance to the drawing room in the house of the Count del Valle de Súchil. This house is located on the northwest corner of the intersection of what are today 20 de Noviembre and Zaragoza streets, and is one of the many structures from this period in Durango that warrant being preserved.[43]

The marriage between Joseph Larrea and Isabel Erauzo produced six children: Ana María, María del Carmen, José María, Isabel, María Josefa and Teresa.[44] Upon reaching adulthood, this generation, just as their forebears, intermarried with a new group of Spaniards, among which notable is Juan Joseph Yandiola y Lexarsa, commander of the Cuerpo de Dragones de San Juan del Río, who married Isabel. When the first Count died, in 1782, his properties were divided up among his children. Ana María, the firstborn, who had married Juan Manuel Castaños, a nobleman from Alcántara, received several of the properties in the Súchil Valley, among them the hacienda Muleros. José María assumed the title of second Count. It is not known which properties were inherited by José María nor why the majority were inherited by his sisters. It is known that he purchased, from Juana Romo de Vivar, in 1792, the hacienda San Miguel de Guatimapé, another vast estate that included Chinacates (today José María Morelos), Boca de San Julián, San Antonio, Santa Teresa de Pinos, San Rafael, Toboso del Norte, Toboso del Sur, Magdalena, Alisos, Torreón, Molino, Santiaguillo, Sauces and Soledad.[45] Because of this, a number of people have erroneously added "de Guatimapé" to the title of Count del Valle de Súchil.

Legend has it that, during a hunting expedition, the second Count was attacked by a bear which resulted in a fistula in his throat which was to plague

38 Archivo de la Catedral de Durango, Libro LXXVII, ff. 197v. y 414. He was paid $27 pesos for having placed some beams in the captiular archives and for repairing a leak in the cathedral, in August, and in December he signed for the payment.

39 Archivo de la Catedral de Durango, Libro LXXVII, f. 212 v. He was paid $4,100 pesos upon finishing the two entrances and a bonus for the two statues above these entrances.

40 Maza, *La ciudad . . .*, p. 23. Here he confirms the crediting of the door to the house of the Count del Valle de Súchil to Pedro de Huertas even though he did not know the name of the architect.

41 Archivo de la Catedral de Durango, Libro LXXVII, f. 339.

42 Bargellini, *La arquitectura . . .*, op. cit., p. 164.

43 According to the census of 1778, p. 278, it was the property of Don Juan Sánz Diez, a businessman. It was described as a "main house, although of one story, of stonemasonry."

44 I am indebted to Miguel Vallebueno for this and the information that follows with regard to the descendants of Joseph Larrea.

45 Hernández, *Durango Gráfico*, p. 30.

him the rest of his life, and which altered his habits. He wandered during the night and slept during the day.[46] Whatever the case may have been, it is certain that his sister Isabel and his brother-in-law Juan Joseph Yandiola were responsible for managing the mining business, the principal source of the family's income. Yandiola also acquired a good number of new haciendas, among them San Isidro de la Punta, formerly the property of the Jesuits in the Guadiana Valley, Labor de Guadalupe, and San Salvador de Horta.[47] With such a quantity of estates, this family, as a whole, was the largest landowner in the southern part of Nueva Vizcaya. The final member of this branch of the family of the Count del Valle de Súchil worthy of note was Guadalupe Yandiola del Campo, the only child of Juan Joseph and Isabel. It was she who sold the house in Durango. Upon her death, in a now-independent Mexico, the Church inherited what remained of her properties.

The amassing of wealth that characterized the life of Joseph del Campo y Larrea ran parallel to the fortunes of the city of Durango. His palatial house is the material expression of this fortune, both of the Count del Valle de Súchil and the capital of the province of Nueva Vizcaya. The subsequent history of the house mirrors the changes in the social and economic life of Durango. Over the years, the building went from being a residence to the scene of exclusively commercial activities. Toward a fuller understanding of the conservation of the house, I will finish with a brief summary of the subsequent owners and the uses to which the house of the Count del Valle de Súchil was put in the nineteenth and twentieth centuries.[48]

During the nineteenth century, the building changed hands several times, exclusively among Germans. Later, it was acquired by Maximilian Damm, also German, a native of Rudolstadt, south of Erfurt in the Thuringia region, who had arrived in Durango in 1850 and had married a Spanish woman whose surname was Palacio.[49] The Damm family conserved the building practically intact between 1858 and 1928, utilizing it as a residence and a store. At the time it was know as the Casa de la Cadena (House of the Chain) because a thick chain had been placed at the entrance. It was later purchased by Calixto Bourillon who kept it for some years until it was acquired, in 1935, by Anacleto García. At that point it was converted into a large warehouse named El Gran Número Once, and it suffered important alterations. It was then that the third flight of stairs, previously mentioned, was added. Additionally, the area comprising the principal courtyard was enlarged, replacing a wall with a row of columns designed to imitate the originals. Above the new columns were placed metal beams to support the upper floor. Toward the end of the 1950s, the house was acquired by Jesús H. Elizondo, a native of Monterrey who had made his fortune in Durango. Prior to its being acquired by Banco Nacional de México, in 1985, a shopping center known as the Plaza los Condes had been established in the building. In 1988, the former house of the Count del Valle de Súchil was restored and adapted to its current use.

46 Ibid. This was represented in a painting by Federico Damm, of Durango, which pertains to a private collection in Durango.

47 "Memoria testamentaria," 15 de agosto de 1799, Archivo de Notarías del Estado de Durango. In addition to the mines at Avino, Yandiola was also involved in those at Yerbabuena and at Ventanas.

48 I am indebted to Luis Sergio Rivera Damm and Miguel Vallebueno for the following information.

49 Saravia, *Apuntes . . .* , op. cit., vol. III, p. 175. Saravia states that before pertaining to Damm, it had been a warehouse known as the Almacén de los Delius.

The Palace of the Count de San Mateo de Valparaíso

Mexico City

The Palace of the Count de San Mateo de Valparaíso

Origins

On the lot granted, in 1523, to Alonso Nortes, cousin of Ginés, who had arrived in the Americas as chief navigator in the armada of Pánfilo de Narváez, was erected an elegant building which was later ordered reconstructed by the Count de San Mateo de Valparaíso, in 1769.

Ignacio González-Polo

The palace of the Count has its origins in the simple and austere house which had been constructed by Juan Cermeño, in 1527. His widow, Ana Martínez, along with her second husband, Diego Pérez de Zamora, undertook improvements on the building, but it wasn't until after the great flood in Mexico City, in 1627, when the subsequent owner, Pedro de Toledo y Mendoza, Chief Carver of the Royal House of Moneda, renovated it, reinforcing the foundations and carefully embellishing its rooms, courtyards and arcades.

The layout of non-ecclesiastical buildings during the period of the viceroyalty, regardless of their size, ornamentation and other factors, were similar in that in order to best serve their purposes, the interior volumes were connected to each other by means of arcades or closed galleries, were of one or more stories and distributed around courtyards. They featured a large entrance vestibule, windows on the ground floor and balconies on the upper floor or floors.

In the seventeenth century, wealthy residents generally lived in independent houses with a mezzanine or second story, the levels divided by a cornice. By this time, the façades had taken on a lighter characteristic than those of the previous century due to the greater number and larger size of the windows, whose jambs tended to extend vertically until reaching the cornices. At the center of the façade was located the grand entrance which included a large door. Above this was generally placed a balcony accessible from the upper level, an evolution of the barred window characteristic of the previous century. This, in turn, was topped by the family's coat of arms.

A carry-over from the sixteenth century was the employment of *tezontle* stone in the dressing of the façades, and the accents and ornamentation continued to be executed in cut *chiluca* quarry stone. Occasionally, glazed ceramic tiles were incorporated, as well as a stucco-like mortar utilized to produce tapestry effects or diverse designs created with bricks which revealed an Andalusian influence.

Houses constructed on corners had the advantage of two exposed volumes and, just as the earlier structures had included fortified towers with battlements on the corners of the roof to aid in the defense of the house, this element continued to be conserved. Although no longer necessary for defense, it provided a pleasant mirador for the residents.

In reality, it wasn't until the eighteenth century that the reserved and austere character of the homes from the sixteenth and seventeenth centuries gave way to structures of great ostentation and openness.

From the descendants of the Chief Carver of the House of Moneda, Pedro de Toledo y Mendoza, the house passed on to Francisco Antonio de Medina y Picazo who acquired it at a public auction, on September 28, 1672, for the sum of $22,200 pesos. He sold it a short time later, in 1683, for $32,000 pesos, plus the taxes owed on the property, to Captain Dámaso de Zaldívar y Retes, a prosperous miner and hacienda owner with vast land holdings in the regions of San Luis Potosí and Zacatecas.

The Count de San Mateo de Valparaíso, Marquis del Jaral de Berrio

The house later came into the hands of a grandson of Captain Dámaso de Zaldívar y Retes, Miguel de Berrio y Zaldívar, who possessed one of the most important fortunes that had been accumulated in New Spain.

His great wealth included more than fifteen haciendas which extended from Cuautitlán to San Luis Potosí, two mining operations in Guanajuato and various urban estates in Mexico City, part of which he had gained through inheritances from his maternal grandmother and from his uncle, the Marquis de San Jorge, wealth which had been administrated and increased in an exemplary manner by his father, Andrés de Berrio.

Through his marriage to Ana María de la Campa y Cos, Ceballos y Villegas, the second Countess de San Mateo de Valparaíso, he acquired his title, originally granted to his father-in-law by Philip V, in 1727.

It wasn't until later, when Miguel de Berrio instituted the *mayorazgo* del Jaral de Berrio, which included his properties within Guanajuato and San Luis Potosí, that he became the Marquis del Jaral de Berrio, a title granted by Charles III on December 18, 1774.

It is noteworthy that the haciendas that constituted the *mayorazgo* and were likewise linked to his title of Marquis, as well as the properties pertaining to his wife, the Countess de San Mateo de Valparaíso, mostly in Zacatecas, formed a continuos range of land that stretched from Durango to Mexico City. As such, his cattle could graze and be driven across the country until reaching one of the provincial capitals or even the slaughterhouses in Mexico City itself, without ever leaving the family's own land.

So prized were the fighting bulls and the horses raised on the haciendas San Mateo de Valparaíso and Jaral that even today there exists a ranch specializing in the raising of fighting bulls that bears the name Valparaíso, and one can still hear spoken the saying, roughly translated, "For the bulls from the Jaral, the horses from there, as well." One of the Count's horses served as a model for Manuel Tolsá's magnificent statue of Charles IV mounted on a steed.

In short, the prestige and economic splendor enjoyed by the Count and the Countess brought them a privileged social and political position.

Don Miguel de Berrio was Chief Mayor and Magistrate of Mexico City, a member of His Majesty's Council in the Royal Tribunal and in the Audience of Accounts of New Spain. Additionally, he was a Captain in the Royal Army and a Knight of the Order of Santiago.

The Countess, for her part, the daughter of Col. Don Fernando de la Campa y Cos, a Knight of the Order of Alcántara, and his second wife, Doña Isabel de Ceballos y Villegas, also contributed to the family patrimony advantageously by way of ten additional haciendas, including Ameca and part of San Mateo de Valparaíso, the family's principal estate, plus another three mining operations, a palace in Zacatecas and a number of important parcels of land within Mexico City.

Thus, in keeping with the luster and magnificence of their position, they decided to reconstruct the house under study here from its foundations. To such end, they commissioned the work to the architect Francisco Antonio Guerrero y Torres. Historically, this was the first building that brought renown to this master builder, one of the best and most original that has graced Mexico City throughout the course of its history.

The Architect
Francisco Guerrero y Torres

If one person can be given credit for Mexico City's once being dubbed "the City of Palaces," it is Francisco Antonio Guerrero y Torres.

With an extraordinary artistic quality that led to his becoming a first-class architect, Guerrero y Torres was the author of such important mansions as the palace under study here, that known today as the Iturbide Palace, that of the Count de Santiago de Calimaya, and that of the *mayorazgo* de Guerrero.

In all of these cases, just as with his exceptional work in the area of religious architecture, such as the Church of the Enseñanza and the Pocito chapel, the artisan did not limit himself to employing his talents only in the designs of the façades in that he was actively involved in the organization of the interior spaces.

It was he who introduced a stylistic change, without breaking from local tradition, taking a firm stand against the *estípite,* reestablishing the use of the column and the pilaster, and promoting a new sensibility in the area of ornamentation, while also transforming the concepts of levels and spaces.

Had it not been for the resounding emergence of the Neoclassical style in

New Spain, it is probable that this master would have founded a school of great stylistic originality by the end of the eighteenth century.

A native of La Villa de Guadalupe (today part of northern Mexico City), he was baptized on February 23, 1727. It was here that he began his career as a journeyman, alongside Ventura de Arellano and working under Manuel Álvarez, José Eduardo de Herrera and Iniesta Vejarano. He received the title of architect on June 20, 1767.

Inventor and builder, named master of the works of the Royal Palace, the Cathedral and the Tribunal of the Inquisition (1774), Guerrero y Torres lacked only the very important title which would have charged him with the city's principal projects, something which would have placed him, for life, at the top of the hierarchy to which an architect could aspire. He was the architect in vogue in New Spain and possessed a clarity that permitted him to interpret the tastes and refinement of the dominant Creole class of the period.

The architect accepted a commission from the Count de San Mateo in 1769, undertaking over the course of ten years, according to him:

> *. . . the construction of his house on the corner of Ángel and Del Rastro streets [today Isabel la Católica and Venustiano Carranza streets]; the storefronts on Zuleta street and the large [house] on the same street; the vaults and dome of the Church of San Bernardo; the bridge at Tula; the small houses of the Coliseo bridge, and the large [house] on San Francisco street.*

As part of his intervention in the first house, the subject of our study here, Guerrero y Torres took advantage of the existing foundation and bearing walls, and reutilized much of the original construction materials. The work commenced on December 5, 1769, and was concluded on May 9, 1772. The cost of the project came to $115,000 pesos.

Unfortunately, when the architect later began construction on "the large house on San Francisco street" which we today know as the Iturbide Palace, he was dismissed by the Count who paid him off, on March 8, 1779, with the sum of $1,000 pesos. The reason was that at his residence, today the headquarters of Banco Nacional de México, the arches and the vault above the vestibule had begun to collapse.

The damage was severe in that "for having erred and because they were collapsing, all three of the large, low arches and all five of the high ones and the area of the vestibule had to be demolished . . . ."

Although Guerrero y Torres wanted to repair the damage, the Count would not consent. As such, the repairs to the house as well as the execution of his plans for the great house on San Francisco street, completed in 1785, were charged to the journeyman Agustín Durán, the architect's brother-in-law.

This was not the worst that Guerrero y Torres was to suffer, however. Although

the triumph of having designed these two magnificent houses cannot be denied, the factor that hurt his career even more deeply than the structural problems at the palace of the Count was having to deal with the illustrious proponents of the Neoclassical movement.

In their zeal to revive the ancient Greco-Roman forms, "they mercilessly applied their straight lines, in the manner of a grille, to the curved lines of the Baroque."

With the establishment of the Academia de San Carlos, in 1782, the battle between the Neoclassical and the Baroque was won. Not only was Baroque painted as being in bad taste but as extravagant, the product of nonsense, ridiculous, disorderly, absurd and rejected by connoisseurs of "good" architecture.

On this subject, José Mangino informed the king that

The lack of submission by the masters of architecture to the rules that prescribe this noble art is the origin of the deformity which can be noted in the public buildings of this capital. Some of them have been raised to a height not allowed by the well-known debility of the ground, with the imminent risk that they be destroyed, and they deprive the adjacent houses of the necessary light, whose residents live in constant fear because they know the grave danger that lies near them. Your Highness has faithful testimony to this truth in the two houses built by the Count de San Mateo on Ángel and San Francisco streets, and the worst is that following his example others have been constructed.

In all of them can be seen neglect in the selection and taste of the decoration of the façades, which is that which constitutes the exterior elegance and beauty of a building, and in many of them one can see with horror a confusion, an unpleasant mixture of the three orders and of others that aren't even known. The doors and windows are placed arbitrarily with neither relationship nor symmetry. The stairways are so dangerous as to be insufferable, and the interior distribution offers neither the rest nor the comfort that was the precise object of their invention.

Finally, one can hardly find a house in which one can distinguish with clarity the different members that should comprise it, and in none of them is one aware in the slightest of the proportion of the whole with its parts and of these to the whole, in which consists the grace of a good construction, whose defects are due to the fact that the professors initiate the work prior to having combined their ideas on paper, because regularly they are unaware of the delineation and geometric design, and it is precisely this lack of combination that causes the general monstrosity of the constructions that disfigure the beautiful streets of this notable capital of the New World, and serve as a ridiculous affair in the eyes of all intelligent men, after having cost their owners enormous sums.

In spite of the foregoing, Guerrero y Torres continued to prosper with such sensational projects as the Santuario de Nuestra Señora de los Ángeles and the Parish

44

y Supromo de Hazienda y Contador Decano

Tribunal y Audiencia De Quentas De este

Miguel de Berrio y Zaldibar Conde de
Comenzo
de 1769.
Se Acabo Mayo
del 1772

Church of San José de México. He was still active when he died, on December 20, 1792, managing to demonstrate his capabilities to the end. One year before his death, his work reached a climax with the beautiful Chapel of the Pocito, on the outskirts of Mexico City, perhaps the only place in which he could work *mere gratis*. It was not only his swan song but, in the words of Justino Fernández, "the exemplary synthesis of old traditions renovated on this earth, to general applause for our taste for the color and the exuberance."

Description of the Palace

Due to its proportion, sobriety, ornamentation and harmony, the house of the Count de San Mateo de Valparaíso is doubtless a fine example of Mexican Baroque architecture from the last third of the eighteenth century. Thus, the building is a source of pride, not only for the institution that occupies it but for the city and the culture that produced it, characterized as it is by its repertoire of a combination of varied elements.

In spite of the alterations that it has suffered, it still conserves, in its façades and interior spaces, a number of details which allow us to appreciate its original majesty. Noted "for its artistic merit," it was designated a National Monument in 1932.

When the building was adapted to house the offices of Banco Nacional de México, in 1884, the mezzanine level was eliminated, leading to a modification of the ground-floor windows which extended their height. From this point onward the building was comprised of two levels, or stories.

At the top of the corner of the building is an element resembling a fortified tower, at the corner of which is located a vaulted niche which houses, flanked by Solomonic columns, a representation of the Virgin. The building's ashlar facing of *tezontle* stone and its moldings of *chiluca* quarry stone are lightly ornamented with mixtilinear forms and it features a peculiar solution in that it is topped not with parapets, as were the majority of mansions from the period, but with forged-iron railing, delimiting the roof-terrace, supported by a series of ornamental pedestal-pinnacles which recall traditional battlements.

During the most recent remodeling, in the twentieth century, the surface area of the structure was considerably enlarged. A new courtyard was added which is an exact copy of the original, and the façade along Isabel la Católica street was extended, incorporating the same design and the identical materials employed in the eighteenth-century construction.

Although it is difficult today to reconstruct the original distribution of the interior spaces due to the modifications necessary to conditioning it to accommodate the needs of a modern banking institution, it should be noted that the present owners of the building have taken great pains to conserve the dignity of the structure, decorating the various offices and public spaces with furniture, paintings and objects which recall the period in which it was occupied by the Count de San Mateo de Valparaíso.

What is certain is that many characteristics still exists which speak of the personality of the architect as well as the peculiar code by which he nourished his professional undertakings.

At this point we to turn to Manuel Toussaint and his personal observations of the building's characteristics:

It is comprised of two courtyards, the principal, with its solemn vestibule, which opens onto Puente del Espíritu Santo street, and the service courtyard, which opens onto Capuchinas street [also known as Ángel]. The principal courtyard, sumptuously decorated, just as are the façades, is notable in that its high arcades are supported by only three arches that intersect at the ends, offering a singular aspect of audacity and lightness. On these arches can be read a legend which tells us the name of the architect: Don Francisco de Guerrero y Torres. At the rear of the courtyard there opens a beautiful portal leading to the staircase; on whose frieze can be seen the construction dates: it commenced on December 5, 1769; it was completed on May 9, 1772.

The staircase, perhaps the most notable element of this monument, is found precisely between the two courtyards, but each has its own entrance or access [to the stairs]. It is, effectively, of double flights, with a helicoid design. It is not a spiral staircase in that it has a central, cylindrical core which serves to support the steps. Nor is it true that one flight leads to the upper floor while the other takes one to the mezzanine; both flights lead to the upper floor and both offer access to the mezzanine level; notable is that one, the flight that is accessed from the principal courtyard leads to the arcades that overlook that courtyard while the other, accessed from the service courtyard, leads to the spaces that overlook the second [courtyard]; perfectly differentiated, they have been accommodated in a single architectural structure, resolving the problem [of the family encountering the service staff] in an admirable manner. A beautiful cupola crowns this monumental staircase, unique in Mexico to my knowledge.

On the upper floor of the house, we have the principal rooms which are difficult to identify at first glance due to the adaptations required by the institution that occupies it today. In some of the more important rooms, some interesting paintings were recently discovered which had decorated the splays of the doors. They depict country scenes and are surrounded by beautiful frames of what seems to be golden plaster. Rather than frescos, they were executed in tempera with which, perhaps, the entire building had been decorated.

To one side of the staircase, the chapel was located, whose remains can be observed in the area which is now occupied by an elevator. The door, which was surely beautiful, has disappeared, and the wall against which the altar had been placed has been opened to provide an access, reducing the former chapel, in order to accommodate the current utilization of space, to a simple passageway. The cupola remains, smaller than the one above the staircase and adjacent to it

when viewed from the roof. On either side of the portal that leads back to the staircase from the area overlooking the principal courtyard is a large vaulted niche in which is located a ceramic water jug which offered refreshment to the house's inhabitants.

The roof, which rather than a parapet has iron railings between the beautiful pinnacles, is a true terrace. There one can admire the two cupolas, dressed with glazed ceramic tiles. And a sudden memory comes to us unexpectedly: the cupolas of the Chapel of the Pocito! They have, effectively, the same shape, equal proportion and are placed in identical relationship to each other. And if we remember that the Chapel of the Pocito, a masterpiece of architecture from the period of the viceroyalty, was also the work of Guerrero y Torres, in 1791, we cannot help but think that the design inspired that work, and although it may not have exactly motivated him, given that in resolving the problem the layout demanded an equal placement regarding the roof, in reality he granted the same admirable appearance to the finishing of the chapel.

The façade of the headquarters of Banco Nacional de México presents us with elegant lines and great sobriety in the distribution of the ornamentation. The ground floor features pilasters with recessed panels framed by undulating molding. The jambs and lintels are simple, with sober molding; the panels that adorn the area above the windows are modern, from when they eliminated the mezzanine. The principal entrance is more sumptuous, the imposts of the pilasters adorned with frames in relief. Above the doorway is a complex, sculpted grouping with vegetal motifs and two angels, in three-quarter relief, which seem to be sustaining the oval medallion which holds the family's coat of arms.

The entrance's segmented arch includes a curious keystone which reaches downward. The enormous keystone divides the two levels as well as provides support for the balconies whose forged-iron railings are supported by robust pies de gallo. The motifs of the ground floor are repeated on the upper floor, the pilasters, with similar ornamentation, again reaching to the height of the cornice, with a convex frieze that is luxuriously sculpted and gargoyles that are supported by small angels which rest on corbels with grotesques, volutes and vegetal motifs. Obeying the arrangement created by the distribution of these gargoyles are the elegant pinnacles which crown the house, between whose bases run the lengths of iron railing of which we have spoken.

At the corner stands the characteristic tower, which is now nothing more than another room with balconies overlooking the two streets, and a niche at its corner. The style of the niche is different than that which marks the rest: it reminds us, with its Solomonic columns and its ornate crowning elements, of the Mexican Baroque of the seventeenth century. The image seems to be of Our Lady of Guadalupe although it lacks the golden splendor that it once must have had.

Finally, in order to get an idea of the distribution and use of the interior spaces of this type of building, Carlos Sánchez, in his book *Memorias de un viejo palacio*, explains:

On the ground floor, at street level, and in the principal courtyard, were to be found the porter's station, the rooms of the coachmen, footmen, groomsmen and the other servants dedicated to the carriages and the horses. In the second were found, generally, the rooms of the servants, attendants and female servants; and in the third, the stables and the storerooms.

On the mezzanine overlooking the principal courtyard were the offices and the living quarters of the employees, and in the second and third, respectively, those of the maids and the personal servants.

On the upper floor and opening onto to the corridors, which were like the arcades around a plaza, were the important rooms. Thus, in the volume which overlooked the principal street and where the projecting balcony was to be found, here were located the [various rooms for receiving guests]; in the gallery opposite this, the chapel, always sumptuous and smelling of incense, and in the volumes on either side the bedrooms of the husband and wife, the bathrooms and the closets.

Some of the Modifications to the Building over the Years

With the death of Manuel Fernández de Córdoba, the last of the descendants of the Count de San Mateo de Valparaíso, who occupied the house until 1867, his heirs sold it to the hacienda owner Clemente Sanz who began to rent it out, after some adaptation work, for diverse uses: a college, a boarding school, a casino, apartments and commercial space, until his daughter, Doña Dolores, sold it to Banco Nacional Mexicana, in 1882. As is well known, upon merging with Banco Mercantil Mexicano, the present-day Banco Nacional de México was formed. This banking institution, after spending $53,000 pesos in renovation work, in 1883, continues to occupy the building today.

The bank closed off the doorways along the street which had provided access to the storefronts and commissioned the architect Ignacio de la Hidalga, son of the celebrated builder of the Teatro Nacional, to make the modifications to the exterior which corresponded to the elimination of the mezzanine, extending the windows upward to the cornice. The great windows which run along the ground floor of the building today are the result of that renovation.

In closing, according to the architect Ortiz Macedo, in the 1930s the surface area of the structure was considerably enlarged with the addition of a new courtyard, an exact copy of the original, and the façade along Isabel la Católica street was extended, as has already been noted.

The Iturbide Palace

Mexico City

The Iturbide Palace

The Houses Preceding the Palace

One of the most famous, beautiful and important streets in Mexico City, beginning in the period of the viceroyalty, is that known today as Francisco I. Madero and which at the time was known as San Francisco, named after the convent which lay along the street. As early as the sixteenth century, it was noted "for its tall and beautiful buildings" as attested to by Francisco Cervantes de Salazar in his work México en 1554.[1]

Martha Fernández

Along this street were to be found the residences of the personages of the highest social and economic strata. In the perspective entitled *Forma y levantado de la ciudad de México,* drawn by the architect Juan Gómez de Trasmonte, in 1628, the stretch of the street where the house of Don Pedro Moncada would later be constructed was lined with one-story houses, characteristic of the residential architecture of the city in that period.

Later, on the site that the Moncada mansion was to occupy in the eighteenth century, a residence was constructed for the Chief Accountant of the viceroyalty, Don Francisco de Córdoba Villafranca, who inaugurated it on the day of Corpus Christi, in the year 1655. The Duchess de Albuquerque, wife of the viceroy, was in attendance and, along with the other guests, observed the religious procession related to this holy day[2] from the central balcony of the house.

About 1670, Don Francisco de Córdoba and his wife, Doña Jesús de Isita, who found themselves without heirs, decided to bequeath their considerable wealth so that it be utilized to found a convent for the Order of Salvador, more commonly known as the Order of Santa Brígida. Although the document regarding the founding of the convent was dated December 24, 1735, after their deaths, their properties came into the hands of the nuns of Santa Brígida, among them the house on San Francisco street.[3]

In the plan of Mexico City executed on a folding screen and entitled *Biombo de los condes de Moctezuma*, painted toward the end of the seventeenth century and attributed to Diego Correa, the house appears represented as an important residence, of two stories, with three courtyards and a flat roof.

1 Cervantes de Salazar, *México . . .*, p. 50.

2 Guijo, *Diario . . .*, vol. II, p. 20.

3 Muriel, *Conventos . . .*, pp. 437-439.

The Construction of the Palace

The nuns of Santa Brígida sold the house to Don Miguel de Berrio y Zaldívar, Count de San Mateo de Valparaíso and Marquis del Jaral de Berrio, and his wife, Doña Ana María de la Campa y Cos, Ceballos y Villegas, who ordered that a luxurious residence be constructed on the site for their daughter María Ana de Berrio, who had married Don Pedro Moncada on January 6, 1768.[4]

The gifts lavished on the young couple by the Count and Countess were splendid, not to mention the promise of a dowry that was to exceed $200,000 pesos and, because María was their only child, direct succession with regard to their wealth and titles.[5]

Don Pedro Moncada was born in Palermo, Sicily, in 1739. Until his adolescence, he lived "in the sumptuous luxury to which the Sicilian princes were accustomed," being of Larderia and Roselini lineage, and held the titles of Count de San Antonio and Marquis de Villafonte. During his youth, in Europe, he resided in nearly all of the courts of the day. He knew Voltaire, Frederick the Great and the Countess du Barry. He came to accept the new liberal, enlightened philosophy and began to be noted for his enormous facility for spending money, a habit that he put into further practice with his arrival in New Spain, in 1764.[6]

Such traits irritated the Marquis del Jaral de Berrio and he never got along with his handsome son-in-law. He and his wife went as far as to withdraw their promise of the dowry to be presented to Don Pedro Moncada.[7] Legend has it that the luxury and magnificence with which the palace on San Francisco street was constructed was a calculated move on the part of the untrusting in-laws who hoped to avoid their fortune falling into the hands of the Sicilian prince.[8]

Work on the palace commenced in 1779, and the architect Francisco Antonio de Guerrero y Torres was charged with the project. With respect to the cost of the construction, two versions exist. One is to be found in an inventory of the Count's possessions after his death, "Relación general de los bienes inventariados por fallecimiento del señor D. Miguel de Berrio y Zaldívar, conde de San Mateo Valparaíso, primer marqués de Xaral de Berrio," in which it is noted that in 1782 the amount spent on the residence had reached "$135,603 pesos and 2 reals, plus $27,688 pesos and 6 reals that were invested later to conclude other details,"[9] which would bring the total amount to $163,291 pesos and 8 reals.

Meanwhile, in documents regarding payments to the builder, "Memorial ajustado de los autos que sigue don Agustín Durán, con la casa mortuoria del señor conde de San Mateo Valparaíso sobre paga de salarios," it is stated that in the execution of the palace the total construction cost was $113,000 pesos.[10]

Whatever the case may have been, it would seem that, in spite of its opulence, the cost of the palace did not equal the $200,000 pesos that had been originally promised to Don Pedro Moncada as a dowry. He moved into the palace when it was finished, in 1785, and resided there until 1800 at which point, now a widower, he returned permanently to Italy.[11]

4 Berlanga Fernández de Córdoba Moncada, "El palacio de Moncada . . . ," pp. 26, 33.

5 Ibid., p. 33.

6 Ibid., pp. 326, 30, 33.

7 Ibid., pp. 34-35.

8 Rivera Cambas, *México . . .* , vol. I, p. 228.

9 "Relación general de los bienes inventariados por fallecimiento del señor D. Miguel de Berrio y Zaldívar, conde de San Mateo Valparaíso, primer marqués de Xaral de Berrio," from the private archives of Guillermo Berlanga Fernández de Córdoba, fs. 122 and 162v., published in: González-Polo, "El arquitecto . . . ," p. 17.

10 "Memorial ajustado de los autos que sigue don Agustín Durán, con la casa mortuoria del señor conde de San Mateo Valparaíso sobre paga de salarios," f. 9, published in: González-Polo, "Memorial . . . ," p. 83.

11 Gurría Lacroix, "Biografía . . . ," p. 76.

12 Ibid.

Don Pedro Moncada and his wife, María Ana de Berrio, had two children: Juan Nepomuceno and María Guadalupe de Moncada y Berrio.[12] It was Juan Nepomuceno de Moncada y Berrio, the third Marquis del Jaral de Berrio, who took over the house when his father left.

In the eighteenth century, the palace was the tallest in the city. It consisted, effectively, of four levels including a ground floor, which included the main entrance and storefronts; a mezzanine where the family offices were located; the upper, or principal, floor where family's private quarters were to be found, including the drawing room, the "canopy" room maintained by titled nobility and the private chapel; and an open, top floor on the roof which featured a loggia composed of a grouping of five arches that served as an overlook which provided a view northward across the Valley of Mexico, then clean and transparent. The loggia was flanked by two rooms constructed to resemble watchtowers and which were utilized, variously, as music rooms, guest bedrooms or, perhaps, as small parlors in which to receive relatives or for informal visits.

There were three courtyards. The principal of these was nearly square and surely tiled. It featured three arcades, on the north, south and west sides of the ground floor, and arcades on the north and south sides of the upper floor. The east and west sides of the upper floor overlooked the courtyard by means of balconies. At the east end of the southern wall was the foot of the principal staircase.

The other two courtyards were located to the south, one directly behind the other, and their composition was much simpler. Within them were to be found the stables, the garages, the laundry facilities, the kitchen, the servants' quarters, and the other service-related spaces.

The façade, although it employed the most commonly used materials from eighteenth-century architecture in Mexico City, *tezontle* stone for the facing and *chiluca* quarry stone for the trim, was at the vanguard from an artistic point of view. Diego Angulo notes the influences of architect Lorenzo Rodríguez as well as those of Francisco Antonio de Guerrero y Torres in the civil architecture that emerged just after the middle of the eighteenth century when he writes that "the entrance of the Mexican house seems to be suffering important alterations in its decoration. The mixtilinear is gaining ground perceptibly and, in a desire to intensify the effect of the richness, bossage is employed on a greater scale; the theme of the valance is also frequent . . . ,"[13] all qualities possessed by this house.

13 Angulo Iñiguez, *Historia . . .*, vol. II, p. 607.

The Transformations in the Nineteenth Century

As mentioned in the foregoing, after Don Pedro Moncada returned to Italy, his son Juan Nepomuceno de Moncada y Berrio lived in the house that had been ordered constructed by his grandfather. Lucas Alamán states that a short time after the Trigarante Army entered Mexico City, on September 27, 1821, and while the palace of the former viceroys was being

17
Banamex

adapted as the residence of Agustín de Iturbide, the future emperor and his wife took up residence in the Moncada mansion.

According to Jorge Gurria Lacroix, some believe that Don Juan Nepomuceno "ceded it graciously" because, perhaps, he held the same liberal ideas as had his father, but his successors claim that "they pressured him to the point where he felt obligated to permit that personage to occupy it." Whatever the facts may have been, the owner of the house had to move his family to the house of his sister, the Marquise de San Román, who was living in the palace of San Mateo de Valparaíso.[14]

Agustín de Iturbide lived in the house until March 26, 1823, and his stay there resulted in the mansion being known, for ever after, as the Iturbide Palace.

Many historic events took place in the house while Iturbide resided there, perhaps the most important revolving around the day he stepped out of the palace, on July 21, 1822, and made his way the several blocks to the Cathedral, where he was crowned Emperor of Mexico.

According to Manuel Rivera Cambas, "the building was improved during this period, adapted to the needs of the personage who inhabited it . . . ."[15] It was at this point when a long list of modifications, alterations, adaptations and restorations began, which were to last until quite recently.

Iturbide vacated the Moncada mansion on March 26, 1823. As Jorge Gurria points out, the palace must have been found to be sad and desolate "after having been the center of political and social life in the country for eighteen months,"[16] but it must also have been deeply worried in that from this point onward its future was uncertain.

In the first place, it is unknown whether Don Juan Nepomuceno de Moncada y Berrio returned to his home after Agustín de Iturbide left.[17] In fact, little is known about the house until 1830, when it was rented to the College of Mining which needed the space while repairs were being conducted on its building by the architect Antonio Villard.[18]

The house was utilized by the College of Mining until 1834, and one must suppose that it underwent further adaptations during this period. It was probably again adapted shortly afterward in that "at the death of the third Marquis del Jaral de Berrio, in 1850, the palace was occupied by government offices."[19]

According to a lithograph by Casimiro Castro, from the middle of the nineteenth century, the only important alteration that can be appreciated on the façade, with the respect to its appearance in its early years, is that the arches of the loggia at the top are seen to be covered with a wooden grating, in the manner of latticework. It is also noteworthy that no signs can be seen in the area of the storefronts, a suggestion that perhaps they had been put to some other use.

14 Gurría Lacroix, op. cit., pp. 81-82.
See also: Alamán, *Historia . . .*, vol. V, pp. 331, 591.

15 Rivera Cambas, op. cit., vol. I, p. 228.

16 Gurría Lacroix, op. cit., p. 96.

17 Ibid., p. 97.

18 Fernández, *El palacio . . .*, p. 38.

19 Gurría Lacroix, op. cit., p. 98.

The Hotel Iturbide

At some point between 1850 and 1852, the Moncada palace was acquired by Don Anselmo Zurutuza, the owner of the Compañía de

Diligencias (stagecoach company) in Mexico City which was located adjacent to the mansion. As such, his plan was to convert it into a hotel which would complement his other business. One of the first things he did was to put together a collection of paintings with which to adorn the public areas of the hotel.[20]

Juan Nepomuceno Almonte, in his *Guía de Forasteros . . .*, from 1852, notes the existence of a restaurant in the "new and very beautiful" Hotel Iturbide, located on San Francisco street and pertaining to the Diligencias company.[21] It is not certain, however, if the building functioned as a hotel immediately in that Zurutuza died, in the city of Puebla, in 1852,[22] and various sources mention that the Hotel Iturbide was opened to the public on March 1, 1855, its proprietor, as well as that of the Compañía de Diligencias, being Don Germán Landa.[23]

During the reign of Emperor Maximilian, the mansion pertained to the brothers Don Antonio and Don Manuel Escandón, who had also acquired what was now known as the Compañía de Diligencias Generales and operated the route between Mexico City and Veracruz. According to Torcuato Luca de Tena, "the palace was then known as the Hotel Iturbide [and] since the coach departed at four in the morning it was necessary to sleep there in order to be punctual for the departure."[24] The Hotel Iturbide seems to have been very luxurious in its time and boasted all the necessary comforts. According to Manuel Orozco y Berra, in 1867 it included

> *five large sections with 170 rooms, which could be connected to form suites of from one to ten rooms. A room with the necessary furniture, clothes cleaned each week and light at bedtime, cost six pesos per month; the luxuriously decorated rooms had a price of from eight to eighty pesos, in such a way that the hotel accommodated all the social strata of the passengers. One of the best restaurants in the city is to be found, a bathhouse, tailor, a bazaar with all types of merchandise, bowling, a maids' room, stables, intelligent servants, an electric bell with which to ring for service, and in a short time gas lighting.*[25]

Certainly, in achieving the appearance of the hotel that Orozco y Berra here describes, the former mansion surely suffered interventions "to give it the form that it presents today, very different than that which it had had before."[26] From photographs taken about 1856 and 1866, we can observe that these changes had not caused a notable difference in the façade in that the number of levels and the ornamental elements present since its construction had been respected. The only evident change is that the windows, including the arches of the loggia, had been provided with wooden shutters.[27]

The interior, on the other hand, seems to have been enlarged. Manuel Orozco y Berra mentioned, in the foregoing, that there were "five large sections." A plan of the Hotel Iturbide, drawn by Kumhardt y Capilla, dated May 5, 1932, shows a building with five courtyards as opposed to the three that the original construction had contained, hence the five sections mentioned by Orozco y Berra. The plan has the shape of a sort of irregular "T" whose longest section extends

20 Ibid.

21 Almonte, *Guía . . .*, p. 458.

22 Novo, "Recuerdos . . . ," p. 104.

23 Orozco y Berra, *Memoria . . .*, p. 230.
Rivera Cambas, op. cit., vol. I, p. 230.

24 Luca de Tena, *Ciudad . . .*, pp. 64-65.

25 Orozco y Berra, op. cit., p. 230-231.

26 Ibid., p. 230.

27 Photographs included in: Tovar de Teresa, *La ciudad . . .*, vol. I, pp. 64-65.

eastward toward what is today Bolívar street, while the west side opens up slightly toward the south. At the same time, the front part of the south courtyard is inclined toward the north.

In the opinion of Rafael Barquero, this expansion most likely occurred when the mansion was converted into a hotel, part of its unification with the stagecoach business. As such, the coaches would arrive via what is today Gante street and carry the passengers to a disembarkation point in the second courtyard. It is possible that the east courtyard was utilized as a garage and the rear courtyard, to the south, as the stables."[28]

28 Rafael Barquero, conversation, October 22, 1993.

To this must be added the fact that the house, as stated by Manuel Orozco y Berra, accommodated 170 rooms, something that would have been impossible given the dimensions of the original structure.

In 1882, the Hotel Iturbide continued to enjoy its reputation as a luxury hotel and now boasted gas lighting.[29] It seems that the alterations continued, however, and Manuel Rivera Cambas mentions that in that same year the façade was "of five floors" as well as five floors on the interior and on which were distributed, according to him, "800 rooms."[30] These statements lead one to conclude that between 1866 (the date of one of the photographs cited in the foregoing) and 1882 another floor must have been added to the building. It is not certain, however, if this new floor extended to the façade since all of the known lithographs and photographs from the period show the building, as seen from San Francisco street, as conserving the original number of levels.

29 Rivera Cambas, op. cit., vol. I, p. 230.

30 Ibid., vol. I, pp. 227, 230.

To this important alteration, if it was actually executed at the time, should be added the fact that the private, family chapel was no longer utilized for such purposes.[31]

31 Ibid., vol. I, p. 230.

At this point, it would appear that after the early adaptations which converted it into a hotel, the former Moncada palace was comprised of a ground floor, with its mezzanine, and three upper levels. The chapel no longer existed, as such, and the grand rooms had been subdivided into hotel rooms and additional rooms distributed around five courtyards.

In 1890, the Hotel Iturbide changed hands. It was acquired by Francisco Iturbe who, in 1899, commissioned the architect Emilio Dondé to undertake a new series of interventions.[32] The three principal changes that the building suffered during this period all involved the principal courtyard.

32 Gurría Lacroix, op. cit., p. 99.

The first was the reinforcement of the west wall, which was found to be in a state of deterioration. According to Samuel Chávez, "the owner wanted to repair it by tearing out the columns and the arches on the ground floor and substituting them with a wall, with the additional objective of being able to establish a greater amount of space on the ground floor, divided into two levels, which could provide a better site for lodging."[33] Fortunately, architect Dondé refused to destroy the arches and sought a solution which would reconcile the interests of the owner and the conservation of the work. This consisted "of constructing a wall which would close off the arcade, but in a way in which the columns would remain affixed to it, and the arches revealed without any alteration; establishing the

33 Chávez, *El Arte . . .*, pp. 4-6.

arcade inscribed into the wall with a series of rectangular doors and circular windows . . . ."[34] Additionally, advantage was taken of the mezzanine level, prolonging it to the point of the arcade, raising "the ceiling to the height of the top part of the door, such that the ground floor was divided into two floors, of which the second floor received light through the round windows that corresponded to it."[35]

34 Ibid.

35 Ibid.

The second important change, in this case from a structural point of view, was the substitution of the base of one of the columns in the courtyard, that which was located "to the left of the entrance on San Francisco street" because it was to be found in a very bad state.[36]

36 Ibid.

Perhaps the most important modification that the building underwent during the intervention by architect Emilio Dondé, however, was the construction of the interior façade of the east side of the courtyard, something that constituted a feat of engineering in that it had to be carried out without risking the structural security of the building. In order to elaborate this new element, according to Samuel Chávez, "a notable amount of shoring up was undertaken, so that little by little the entire façade was replaced from the base up, without destroying the original rather in adjacent parts that were substituted gradually by the new construction."[37]

37 Ibid.

In this fashion, from the three arcades of the interior façades of the ground floor that the original mansion had possessed, thanks to architect Dondé there were now four, the structural layout which remains today.

In spite of the passage of time, by the end of the nineteenth century the Hotel Iturbide still enjoyed "the most fortunate and privileged location," according to Salvador Novo. It was still neighbor to some of the most prestigious palaces, "the most aristocratic part and street in the city: Plateros and San Francisco [streets]." Moreover, as Novo recounts, "the Hotel Iturbide was just around the corner from the grand Teatro Nacional, whose Neoclassical majesty lorded over Vergara street (today Bolívar) at the point where the then residential and Pompeian and broad Cinco de Mayo avenue terminated."[38]

38 Novo, op. cit., p. 106.

In photographs from the beginning of the twentieth century, we can appreciate the façade of the hotel, with its original distribution of levels and its windows, as well as the arches of the loggia, covered by wooden shutters, as was observed in the earlier photographs. From the entrance hangs an electric light fixture, at the time certainly the latest in technological advances, and among the storefronts can be observed two businesses: Iturbide Curio Stores and J. F. Dreinmofer.

In the principal courtyard can be appreciated the arches on the east and west sides, now closed off and with wooden doors topped by fan windows with glass in the shape of flower petals. From the ceiling hang electric light fixtures.

As late as the 1930s, the four rear courtyards of the hotel existed. The one to the west, which was accessed from Gante street, was reached through a semicircular arch with square indentations, supported by jambs with the same ornamentation. The remaining openings featured architraves with frames of quarry stone and balconies on the upper level. It was comprised of two floors plus a mezzanine. From here there was access to the central service courtyard through another semicircular arch supported by jambs which featured bands of quarry stone.

The central service courtyard was surrounded by three levels, the first including a mezzanine. The windows of the uppermost floor were topped with architraves, framed with quarry stone and featured balconies which ran the length of the walls. This courtyard was connected to the east courtyard via an opening with architrave and a passageway with a wooden roof. Access to the west courtyard, on the other hand, was via a semicircular arch topped by a fan window fashioned from wrought iron which also served to safeguard people walking along the mezzanine level.[39] In the plan drawn by Kumhardt y Capilla, mentioned earlier and corresponding to the year 1932, one can observe that the hotel had adopted other technological advances. The bathrooms were moved to make way for the elevators that Salvador Novo remembers in this always modern hotel, and the first Lady Baltimore cafe in Mexico was housed here, which created stiff competition for the Sanborns restaurant, at the time still located in a small storefront at 10 Madero street.[40]

39 Photographs provided by Rafael Barquero, to whose kindness I am indebted.

40 Novo, op. cit., p. 115.

The Revaluation in the Twentieth Century

Given the building's qualities, especially with regard to those of its façade and its central courtyard, as well as the historic events associated with the site, the Iturbide Palace was declared a National Monument on February 9, 1930,[41] although this designation did not impede the modifications by which the building continued to be readapted to the needs of the of the new century.

Although it is commonly believed that the retail corridor Pasaje Bolívar, which traverses the entire block and whose construction eliminated the four rear service courtyards of the hotel, was constructed in 1930,[42] the plan of the Hotel Iturbide drawn by Kumhardt y Capilla, mentioned in the foregoing, indicates that on May 5, 1932, the date which the plan bears, the hotel still existed in its earlier condition and the Pasaje Bolívar had not yet been opened.

It was apparently a bit later when the corridor was constructed, which connected Bolívar and Gante streets, after which the palace conserved only its principal courtyard. Of the other four sections, only remnants are to be found in the area above the ceiling of the corridor.

Meanwhile, what remained of the former hotel was given over to offices and commercial establishments,[43] uses to which it remained dedicated until 1965 when Don Agustín Legorreta promoted its rescue on behalf of Banco Nacional de México. Legorreta himself explained the circumstances, in 1972, in the following manner: "[S]ome years ago we at Banco Nacional de México learned that the owner of this beautiful building wished to sell it as he considered that the income it was producing for him was not in balance with its location, and he did not have the resources necessary for its restoration. The board of directors of the bank made the decision to acquire the Iturbide Palace and to, in the future, utilize it to house Crédito Bursátil, today Financiera Banamex. The board felt that the size, location and presence of the building made it a site worthy of becoming home to one of the most important credit institutions in the country while at the same time it

41 *Catálogo Nacional de Monumentos . . .*, vol. III, p. 1335.

42 Gurría Lacroix, op. cit., p. 100.
Catálogo Nacional de Monumentos . . ., op. cit., vol. III, p. 1336.

43 Gurría Lacroix, op. cit, p. 100.

served as an added symbol of the bank's colonial character."[44]

Naturally, in order to fulfill its new functions, the Iturbide Palace had to be submitted to new adaptation work, a project which lasted from 1963 until 1972 and was carried out by the architect Ricardo Legorreta, in consultation with a committee which included Dr. Francisco de la Maza and the architects Gonzalo Garita and Ricardo de Robina.[45]

Ricardo Legorreta explained the criteria which guided the project as follows:

> *[G]iven the state in which the palace was to be found and the modifications it had suffered, it was decided to free it of all of the added elements which were not original while leaving some of the modifications undertaken by architect Dondé toward the end of the last century, not only because they had been carried out with very good judgment and excellently executed, but because eliminating them would involve substantial modification to the building.*[46]

The work undertaken on the building can be separated into two categories: the elements that were eliminated and those which were constructed. Within the first category are the various levels of flooring which were removed in order to recover the original level, the roof over the courtyard and, of course, the uppermost floor. The lofts that had been constructed beneath the arcades by shopkeepers and merchants were removed as well as was the staircase and the elevator.

New construction included a new staircase, new elevators and a new covering for the building, of a convex shape, which allowed taking advantage of the space on what had originally been the roof. Doors, tiling and other minor elements were replaced without attempting to imitate the originals. To complete the idea of an aesthetic whole, furnishings where selected which complemented the characteristics of the original palace.[47]

After the restoration work, the Iturbide Palace was to be found with the form and characteristics by which we know it today, apart from some minor interventions carried out by architect Ricardo Prado in the 1980s.

44 Legorreta, "Prólogo," pp. 7-8.

45 Ibid., pp. 10-11.

46 Legorreta, "Criterio . . . ," p. 119.

47 Ibid., pp. 119, 122-123. Legorreta, "Prólogo," op. cit., pp. 11-12.

The Architects of the Iturbide Palace

As the reader is well aware by this point, the Iturbide Palace, as it is known today, is not the work of a single architect. Rather, it is the sum total of centuries of work and the creativity of various artists. In all fairness, however, full credit must be given to the project developed by Francisco Antonio de Guerrero y Torres, which was executed by Agustín Durán, in that they were, after all, the authors of the original building on which the subsequent architects were to intervene.

Diego Angulo holds that the Iturbide Palace is possibly the masterpiece of domestic architecture from the entire period of the viceroyalty.[48] As such, in order to more fully understand the work, it is important to look more closely at its creators.

By the time Francisco Antonio de Guerrero y Torres had accepted the commission from the Marquis del Jaral de Berrio to construct the palace on San Francisco street, he was already a recognized architect, in 1774 having been granted the post of Chief Master of the Cathedral and the Royal Palace in Mexico City.[49] Additionally, it would seem that he had become the trusted architect of the Marquis, for whom he had executed a number of works beginning in 1769.[50]

On March 8, 1779, however, when the ground floor of the palace on San Francisco street had barely been raised, the Marquis del Jaral de Berrio dismissed Francisco Antonio de Guerrero y Torres because "the arches and vaults of the vestibule [of the house on] the corner of Ángel and El Espíritu Santo" had collapsed.[51] This, of course, was the home of the Count of San Mateo de Valparaíso, Marquis del Jaral de Berrio, and his wife, and even though the architect offered to pay for the damages, "the Count did not consent, rather he paid him in full what was owed him up until that day."[52]

After his dismissal, Guerrero y Torres was replaced by his brother-in-law, Agustín Durán. This man, apart from being the brother of the architect's wife, Doña Ana Sofía, had worked as a journeyman since at least 1769, when he worked for nineteen weeks, beginning in March of that year, alongside Guerrero y Torres "in the repair work on the cracks in the church of the Sagrario of the Metropolitan Cathedral, earning one real per day . . . ."[53]

It would seem, however, that Agustín Durán was not a titled architect.[54] In spite of this, after the departure of Guerrero y Torres, he took charge of all of the projects pertaining to the Marquis del Jaral de Berrio. In the aforementioned "Memorial ajustado . . . ," which records the relationship between Durán and the Marquis del Jaral de Berrio in terms of the salary paid him, it is noted that "he satisfactorily put . . . the vault of the convent church of San Bernardo," was in charge of the construction of the house on Coliseo street and that "he demonstrated his intelligence regarding architecture, for the construction of the magnificent houses on Ángel, Zuleta street [and that on] San Francisco . . . ."[55] All of these had been previously designed by Francisco Antonio de Guerrero y Torres.

Ignacio González Polo believes that perhaps the most well-known intervention by Agustín Durán was the design of "some plans and budgets, revised by the Academia de San Carlos, for the celebrated structure which was the Alhóndiga (public granary) in the city of Guadalajara (1796), attributed to a master builder named Agustín Alejandro Durán y Villaseñor. The work was completed, in 1809, by another architect, José del Mazo y Avilés."[56]

After having completed the work on the house on San Francisco street, Agustín Durán attempted to bill his work as "master" of the project and not just as a journeyman, eventually filing a lawsuit of which there is a record, from 1785, in the "Memorial ajustado . . . ." that has been referred to herein. By this point, the Marquis del Jaral de Berrio had died, but his estate responded to the suit by

48 Angulo Iñiguez, *Historia* . . . , (1945-50), op. cit, vol. II, p. 601.

49 Castro Morales, "Los maestros . . . ," p. 143.

50 González-Polo, "Los palacios . . . ," p. 14.

51 The first to reveal the facts behind the dismissal of Guerrero y Torres was Heinrich Berlin ("Three Master . . . ," p. 381).
For more information on the subject, see: González-Polo, "Los palacios . . . ," op. cit., p. 15 and González-Polo, "Memorial . . . ," op. cit., pp. 79-96.

52 "Memorial ajustado . . . ." f. 32 vta., cuaderno 3°, published in: González-Polo, "Memorial . . . ," op. cit., p. 90.

53 Archivo General de la Nación, *Bienes Nacionales*; 1023, doc. 81. (Published by González Franco, et al in: "Notas . . . ," p. 98).

54 Memorial ajustado . . . ." fol. 2 v, cuaderno 2°, published in: González-Polo, "Memorial . . . ," op. cit., p. 92.

55 Ibid., pp. 82-83. The house on Coliseo are the present-day nos. 3 and 4 Bolívar street while the house on Zuleta street is, today, no. 1 Venustiano Carranza street.

56 González-Polo, "Memorial . . . ," op. cit., p. 80.

Durán claiming that none of the projects carried out for the Marquis "were his works, rather the mere execution of what had already been designed, prepared and delineated by the master Don Francisco Guerrero y Torres, which is what all journeymen do."[57]

This response is partially justified in that, according to María del Carmen Olvera Calvo and Ana Eugenia Reyes y Cabañas, the journeymen were "who were in charge of the so-called 'work crews,' that is, they were responsible for directing the tradesmen and the laborers and their activities, they themselves directed by the architect, engineer or master."[58] In the case of Agustín Durán, however, faced with the absence of the master Guerrero y Torres, he was forced to take charge of the project and, apart from assigning duties, controlling the time frames, checking calculations, etc., he was responsible, effectively, for all of the aspects normally pertaining to a master.

As such, the architect José del Mazo y Avilés sent a document, signed by him and dated April 14, 1785, in which he made an "adjustment" to the fee so that it corresponded to the customary amount, although no rate had been established, paid to an architect "for the direction of constructions and according to its type . . . ." Del Mazo y Avilés concludes by stating that the compensation that corresponded to the direction "of the construction of the two houses that were for the Count de San Mateo, one on San Francisco street and the other on Coliseo street is deemed to be worth fifteen pesos weekly, which in the span of six years totals $4,680 pesos and that it is the least, with respect to the good construction and beauty of San Francisco street . . . ."

To this must be added a declaration included in the same "Memorial ajustado . . . ." which included the lawsuit brought by Agustín Durán. Don José Gorráez stated "that Durán, with the exception of one or another thing that he executed alone, directed to completion said construction according to the plan left by the master Torres."[59]

As Diego Angulo correctly pointed out, although there exists "no more testimony of the authorship by Guerrero than that of his style, this would seem sufficiently valuable in being able to attribute it to him with a great degree of certainty."[60] In other words, although there is no documentation which confirms that it was Guerrero y Torres who designed the project for the construction of the Moncada palace, it is sufficient only to observe its characteristics in order to attribute it to him.

We cannot, however, make light of the merits of Agustín Durán in the execution of the work, not only carrying out the plans created by Guerrero y Torres but, perhaps, even more as suggested by the unsettling shift in the "Memorial ajustado . . . ." whereby it begins by insisting that Durán had done nothing more that follow the plans of Guerrero y Torres yet concludes by accepting that Durán "alone" executed "one or another thing," to which was annexed the document signed by José del Mazo y Avilés which practically attributes "the good construction and beauty" of the palace to Durán.

57 González-Polo, "Memorial . . . ," op. cit., p. 86.

58 Olvera Calvo and Reyes y Cabañas, "La importancia . . . ," p. 98.

59 González-Polo, "Memorial . . . ," op. cit., p. 82.

60 Angulo Iñiguez, *Historia* . . . . (1945-50), op. cit., vol. II, pp. 602-603.

Much remains to be researched regarding this topic, but given the documental evidence uncovered at this point we can affirm that the Moncada palace was created and constructed by two architects: Francisco Antonio de Guerrero y Torres and Agustín Durán, whose work was later complemented by Emilio Dondé, Ricardo Legorreta and Ricardo Prado.

The Iturbide Palace Today

A Formal Reading

After all of the enlargement and mutilation suffered by the Moncada palace over the years, what remains conserved today is the façade and a courtyard around which rise three floors, plus the mezzanine forming part of the ground floor. It occupies a nearly square lot, with a single entrance on the south side of what today is Francisco I. Madero street.

The façade is truly rich and spectacular. Today, its original proportions have been partly lost in that there are windows in the openings which had originally been the doors which provided access to the storefronts. This does not, however, impede our appreciation of its three primordial characteristics: the upward aspiration, the great movement and the ornamental richness.

The area of the façade comprising the ground, mezzanine and second floors is divided into vertical sections in which fenestration alternates with solid wall. Each section is demarcated by pilasters of *chiluca* quarry stone which, in the case of the windows, form jambs that rise to the height of the cornice. On the ground-mezzanine level, the pilasters feature powerful moldings while those of the entrance area and the second floor are profusely ornamented with natural elements. All of the windows were actually doors that opened onto balconies, accentuating the upward aspiration.

The areas of solid wall are dressed with ashlars of *tezontle* stone and framed by *chiluca* ornamented with frets, on the ground and mezzanine levels, and by interlaced and ornamented circles on the second floor. These frames also serve to call attention to the reliefs which decorate eight of the panels.

The broadest of these vertical sections are those at each end and the one at the center. In the former two, against the panels of *tezontle*, are enormous medallions which at one time featured coats of arms while the one at the center comprises the entrance portal and, above it, the balcony which was accessed from the drawing room.

The third floor likewise contributed, especially at the beginning, to the building's sensation of upward aspiration. The watchtowers, each with a pair of windows, marked the corners of the house while the grouping of five arches which formed the overlook (today filled in as windows) drew all eyes upward. These depressed arches are supported by pilasters which include imbedded columns, above which, between the rich ornamentation of the spandrels are young atlantes which support gargoyles.

Above the cornice at the top are a series of inverted arches crowned by finials while atop the watchtowers is molding of irregular lines that include small volutes.

One of the most outstanding features of the façade, however, is the sensation of movement produce by the creation of independent units with distinct characteristics, such as the unification of the pairs of windows at the mezzanine level, each with its valance beneath, through the incorporation of a continuous balcony railing, and the grouping of arches at the top framed by the watchtowers. The relative sobriety of the second floor contrasts with the colonnade above it and the compositional and ornamental richness of the ground and mezzanine levels below. Another factor is that while there are eight windows on the ground floor, the mezzanine contains only four and the second floor five.

The rich ornamentation of the palace begins with the diversity of decorative motifs. The geometric motifs, based on the mixtilinear molding, which dominate the ground floor and mezzanine contrast with those of a natural character which are found on the valances, on the quarry-stone pilasters of the second floor and on the spandrels of the arches of the overlook and the entrance. To these motifs are added reliefs, escutcheons and *rocaille* ornamentation.

The entrance merits a detailed description. The doorway is topped by a basket-handle arch of multiple moldings and is lightly flared, granting it depth. The arch is supported by jambs, without imposts, whose molding is a continuation of that of the arch. The doorway is flanked by pilasters of the Ionic order which rest on bases decorated with molding that forms geometric figures.

The pilasters are decorated with mixtilinear moldings which run the entire length of the shafts and which serve to frame profuse ornamentation of a naturalistic character which includes *rocaille* elements, flowers, fruit, mermaids, twin-tailed canephoroe, lions' heads from whose mouths emerge draperies that, through a complex foreshortening, seem to be tugged at by small putti.

An enormous valance extends from the cornice to the keystone of the arch, at the center of which is a panel covered with dense foliage which supports a human head nestled in a scallop-shaped molding. This is surrounded by rich and irregular ornamentation composed of *rocaille*, leaves and knots. The valance is flanked by a pair of youths, of great size, each standing on a pedestal of leaves.

Passing through the entrance, one arrives in the vestibule that is topped by a barrel vault which is clearly divided into six sections by ribs decorated with moldings which form geometric figures and which are united at the center by a molded panel in the form of a star.

The arch which separates the vestibule from the courtyard is semicircular and is supported by faceted jambs which rest on paneled bases. Arch and jambs are ornamented with multiple, thick moldings which form geometric figures.

The courtyard, as mentioned in the foregoing, is nearly square in shape. Originally, only three of the sides were arcaded but, after the intervention by Emilio Dondé, all four sides feature arcades at the level of the ground floor while on the second floor only the north and south sides have arcades, as was the case of the original mansion.

The arches on the ground floor are semicircular while those on the second floor are depressed. They are supported by slim columns of the Doric order with smooth shafts and whose tall bases are ornamented with moldings that form geometric figures. At the corners of the courtyard, the columns unite and produce the effect of a triple column. The area above the arches is filled with a rich ornamentation of foliage. The spandrels of the ground floor contain wreathed medallions within which are to be found portraits of unknown personages crowned with laurel leaves while the spandrels of the second floor feature volutes on which stand young atlantes who support waterspouts in the form of dolphins.

All of the balcony entrances which overlook the courtyard are surrounded by broad frames of *chiluca*, with moldings forming geometric figures, whose jambs rise to the level of the cornice, thereby forming panels between the lintel and the cornice.

In the southeast corner of the courtyard is the staircase. At its foot, on the ground floor, there are two semicircular arches supported by jambs with no imposts, plus a third, rectangular opening, with architrave, which is separated from the other two by an embedded column. The arches, their jambs, the base of the column and the rectangular opening are all ornamented with moldings that form geometric figures. This staircase was designed by architect Ricardo Legorreta.

Even more outstanding is the access to the staircase on the second, principal floor. It is comprised of three semicircular arches supported by jambs onto which have been placed fluted *estípite* pilasters with Ionic capitals. The extrados of the arches are flared and the small spandrels are ornamented with foliage.

In the southwest corner of the second floor lies what once had been the family's private chapel. The entrance is richly ornamented. It features an architrave, and the jambs and lintel are decorated with a motif based on leaves. At the center of the lintel is a pedestal, in the form of a valance and ornamented with thick foliage, which serves to support a sculpted image of the Virgin of Guadalupe. Above her is a canopy formed by a large crown from which hangs draperies, held open by a pair of angels who rest on volutes which project from the architrave.

The relief of the Virgin covers the entire height of the entablature. In order to balance the composition there are two pairs of decorative elements which flank the central motif, and above it is a sculpted relief flanked by two large cherubs.

In the spaces between the sculptural elements, along the frieze, are four elements from the Litany of Our Lady of Loreto: the Tower of David, the Fountain of Grace, the Seat of Wisdom and the Gate of Heaven.

The area above the cornice is exquisite, featuring a pair of volutes on which the aforementioned cherubs sit, framing an enormous valance, of multiple points, at the center of which is the face of an angel surrounded by foliage and volutes. At each end of this sculptural grouping is an ornamented pinnacle.

The shape of the chapel is rectangular while its roof is composed of two elliptical apses, opposite each other, which rise from the ornamented cornice. Within each of these is molding in the shape of a scallop. Between the apses is an octagonal cornice, equally ornamented, which serves as the support for the cupola. The springing of the arches which rise to the octagon are comprised of corbels which support angelic atlantes.

The cupola lacks a supporting wall and is found divided into eight sections, on each of which is a window, double-lobed and splayed. Seen from the roof, the cupola features a simulated supporting wall, where the windows open, topped by a powerful projecting cornice. The dome is covered by glazed ceramic tiles. The lantern above it is comprised of three openings alternating with three niches, also with a projecting cornice and topped by a small cupola.

The Palace's Stylistic Affiliation

The compositional and ornamental richness of the Iturbide Palace has awakened the interest of specialists who, in an attempt to understand it, have looked for possible models which might have existed in the period of its construction.

Diego Angulo, for example, believes that the overlook, with its five arches flanked by the *faux* watchtowers, "might bring to mind the remote model of Monterrey in Salamanca as in the drawing of the house of Cortés in the Archive of the Indies" while the medallions on each end of the façade seem, to him, to have been inspired by the customs building in Mexico City.[61]

61 Ibid., vol. II, pp. 601-602.

For his part, Carlos Flores Marini feels that the "exaggerated slimness" of the columns in the courtyard "give it an Italianate vision which, on the other hand, borders on the reckless given the characteristics of the subsoil of our city."[62]

62 Flores Marini, "El Palacio . . . ," p. 63.

The generalized opinion is that Don Pedro Moncada took charge of the supervision of the construction of the palace "with the desire that it resemble to some degree the royal palace in Palermo, and that of his ancestors the princes of Larderia."[63]

63 Berlanga Fernández de Córdoba Moncada, op. cit., p. 34. González-Polo, "Los palacios . . . ," op. cit., p. 17. Flores Marini, op. cit., p. 63. *Catálogo Nacional de Monumentos* . . . , op. cit., vol. III, p. 1336.

In contrast to this belief exists a declaration by the Countess de San Mateo de Valparaíso in which she affirms that when the architect Francisco Antonio Guerrero y Torres was dismissed from the project, it was directed "by the Count himself," her husband.[64] At no point does she mention the participation of Don Pedro Moncada.

64 González-Polo, "Memorial . . . ," op. cit., p. 95.

We must also remember the antipathy which the Marquis del Jaral de Berrio held with regard to his son-in-law, something that would have made it quite difficult for the Marquis to allow him to intervene in the construction of a palace that he himself was paying for.

Additionally, according to a biography written by Guillermo Berlanga Fernández de Córdoba Moncada, during the construction of the palace Don Pedro Moncada, his wife and children "nearly always" resided in the city of Puebla."[65]

65 Berlanga Fernández de Córdoba Moncada, op. cit., pp. 34-35.

From a formal point of view, the only resemblance between the courtyard of the royal palace in Palermo and that of the Iturbide Palace is the presence of tall, slim columns which, more than a concrete relationship with the former, reminds us, as pointed out by Carlos Flores Marini, in a more general way of the Italian palaces from the period of the Renaissance. The differences between the palaces

in Mexico City and Palermo are far more numerous than the similarities given the temporal distance that separates them. The palatine courtyard of the latter was constructed in the early years of the seventeenth century by the Viceroy Duke de Maqueda,[66] and can be classified as being of the Mannerist style, while the courtyard of the house in New Spain, under study here, is Baroque, the one in Palermo lacking completely the decorative-symbolic program that forms part of the artistic personality of the Iturbide Palace.

66 *Sicilia* IV, p. 38.

This palace responds to the concrete characteristics of the art of New Spain from the eighteenth century. Manuel Rivera Cambas clarified, in 1882, that "one of the most beautiful architectural works in the capital pertains to the genre of Churrigueresque and therefore is not subject to a determined order, participating in all of them at the same time,"[67] and in a certain way he is right.

67 Rivera Cambas, op. cit., vol. I, p. 227.

Today, the Iturbide Palace is considered a Baroque architectural work, forming part of a modality within the Baroque of New Spain known as *neostilo*. According to Jorge Alberto Manrique, the originator of this term, the *neostilo* constitutes the "last gasp of Mexican Baroque" and its most important characteristic is the return to the use of the column (hence the name) and the pilaster (excluding the *estípite*). Although a modality of Baroque, it is different from the other Baroque modalities that appeared in New Spain. Its novelty lies, principally, in that it employed the oldest forms from the traditional architecture in New Spain while granting them new feeling and, at the same time, introducing new resources.

Thus, within its repertoire are included the most famous and significant devices utilized in the art of New Spain, such as Classical columns with smooth shafts or with zigzagging or undulating striation, Solomonic columns and ornamented pilasters. Also reemployed were mixtilinear bossage, valances, foliage from the Solomonic modality of Baroque, carving characteristic of the *estípite* modality of Baroque, and Rococo ornamentation, among others.

Being the new modality that it was, it also "invented elements or structures that have no direct antecedent in our country" such as "the daring use that is made of moldings," the creation of façades and *retablos* of symmetrical composition and the employment of Baroque space distribution.[68]

68 Manrique, "El 'neóstilo' . . . ," pp. 335-367.

After so much review and research, from my point of view, the *neostilo* was the manner in which the Baroque artists in New Spain interpreted and put into practice the ideas emerging from the Enlightenment. It was, certainly, the last gasp of Baroque in New Spain, but it was likewise the first artistic manifestation of the Enlightenment in the country.[69] From here its great importance emerged and with it, of course, the Iturbide Palace.

69 Fernández, "El 'neóstilo' . . . ."

As we have seen, this building employs more than one of the characteristics that can be identified as *neostilo*: the movement in the façade, the ornamented pilasters at the entrance, the columns of smooth shafts in the courtyard, the presence of valances and *rocaille* ornamentation and, most of all, the insistent inclusion of the moldings which form geometric figures and violent chiaroscuro contrasts.

The inclusion of elements within wreathed medallions, reminiscent of the Renaissance, and the union of the columns in the corners of the courtyard, of clear Gothic origin, also form part of this reaching into the past for solutions, resulting in an almost encyclopedic inventory which was characteristic of the Enlightenment at this point in history, the *neostilo* becoming one of its architectural manifestations.

If, from a formal point of view, the Iturbide Palace can be considered a work linked to the Enlightenment, of no less importance is the iconographic program that it contains.

An Iconographic Reading

The entrance to the palace seems to allude to the honors that New Spain and its residents granted the noble owners of the house. This can be explained from a social point of view if we consider the strict stratification of the period in which the aristocracy occupied the highest level of a well-defined pyramid. As such, on the jambs of the entrance there appear canephoroe who carry the fruits of the earth in their baskets, as if an offering to the noble blood of the owners.

Above the arch, two scantily clad youths, who hold maces, appear to represent modern "savages," similar to the athletic personages of classical mythology, perhaps an allusion to the indigenous peoples of New Spain, now subjects of the Crown of Spain and vassals of a family of nobles.

This symbology is completed, at either end of the façade, by the large medallions, today devoid of ornamentation but which once surely held the coats of arms of the Crown of Spain and those of the Marquis del Jaral de Berrio and the Count de San Mateo de Valparaíso or, perhaps, that of one of the noble forebears or relatives of Don Pedro Moncada.

The rest of the iconographic program of the façade is constituted by two series of reliefs which are distributed among the large panels of *tezontle*, at the mezzanine level and at the level of the second floor. The first series represents the abductions from Greek mythology and are placed in the following order: to the east of the entrance is the abduction of Ganymede and, to the west, that of Persephone, next to which is the abduction of Europa and, on the opposite side, that of Helen.

In the relief allusive to the abduction of Ganymede can be appreciated the moment in which the adolescent is transported by an eagle, the favorite animal of Zeus, to Olympus.

Persephone appears tied at the waist by her abductor, her uncle Hades, brother of Zeus and lord of the underworld. He holds a pomegranate above his head which alludes to the story of how she broke her fast while in the underworld and, upon eating the pomegranate, became forever chained to this realm.

The abduction of Europa is represented in its most well-known form in which Zeus transforms himself into a bull and Europa, after overcoming her fear of the animal, mounts him, at which point Zeus seizes the opportunity and leaps into the sea with the maiden on his back, making his way to Crete.

In the relief allusive to the abduction of Helen, we can observe the story in which Paris carries off the daughter of Zeus, on a ship, to Troy. The keel of the ship is represented by a volute.[70]

70 I wish to thank Dr. Gustavo Curiel, Elena I. Estrada de Gerlero, the architect Manuel González Galván and Edgardo Ganado Kim for their collaboration on the research into the iconography of the palace.
Grimal, *Diccionario* . . . .
Grimal, et al., *Mitologías* . . . .
Selman, *Mitología* . . . .

In the reliefs found at the level of the second floor, the ravages of time have done much to erase their attributes, including parts of the figures, making their identification difficult. Hypothetically, the following identification can be proposed: the relief to the east of the central balcony seems to represent Architecture while that to the left, Wisdom. Next to the former is what appears to be Agriculture and, on the opposite side, Astronomy.

Architecture is the best conserved of the four and its iconography seems clear. There is a Tuscan column at the center, flanked by a seated woman and small boy, standing. The woman holds a compass and a sphere while the boy holds a square. From the column hangs a plumb. Both the plumb and the compass are also symbols of Geometry, the plumb representing the movement, time and gravity of bodies, and the compass representing line, surface and depth. In this case, however, they are put to the service of Architecture in that within it are combined the knowledge of Geometry and Arithmetic.

Wisdom is also represented by two human figures, again a seated woman and a young boy standing. The woman looks skyward, toward the source of light, and bears a representation of the sun on her chest. It is common to relate Wisdom with Philosophy since the latter "is a word which signifies no less that a Love for Wisdom . . . ," and it is commonly considered the branch of knowledge which contains all of the others.

Agriculture appears in the relief on the Iturbide Palace represented by a young boy who holds a scythe and an ax or mattock. Its inclusion in the series makes sense in that Agriculture is "the art of working the land, seeding, planting and knowing the condition of plants and trees, observing the appropriate times, necessities and places."

The relief which I believe represents Astronomy is the most eroded and damaged of the four. The figure has lost part of its head as well as both hands, leaving as the only surviving element a sphere, perhaps the earth, supported on a base whose members are so close together as to give the impression of a pillar. The incorporation of the celestial sphere in Astronomy is explained "by being its specific objective the measurement of the heavens and the consideration of its ordered movements."[71]

71 Ripa, *Iconología* . . . .

I understand the iconographic sense of the façade as follows. All of the abductions are related to Zeus, the most important god on Olympus as well as the most powerful. The other reliefs represent, as a whole, wisdom in that to construct, to work the land, to cultivate thought and to reach for an understanding of the heavens are all elements of same. Thus, power and wisdom are related to both the Crown of Spain and the owners of the palace, whose coats of arms flanked and delimited the walls of the façade. This would also explain the offerings that it would seem were being made by the natives of this land, justified by the elevated virtues of Crown and owners.

Within the spandrels of the arches in the courtyard, as mentioned in the foregoing, are portraits of personages with crowns of laurel. Various hypotheses may be proposed relative to these figures. What is clear is that they seem to allude to the Classical world but, in an attempt to go a step beyond, we might consider them, with their laurel, to be poets, an idea that can be reinforced by the fact that it was poets who sang of classical mythology and specified the liberal and mechanical arts, and by extension the interior world of the house and the daily lives of its inhabitants can be related to the image projected to the exterior world via the palace's façade.

With respect to the presence of profane iconography, especially that related to classical mythology, in the art of New Spain, it is not unusual to find numerous examples of such which date as far back as the sixteenth century. Its appearance in the Baroque world has been explained by Francisco de la Maza "as a rest from the constant and devout religiosity that accompanied from sunup to sundown"[72] the society of the period. To this might be added the existence of Enlightened thought that was gaining prominence at the point in which the Iturbide Palace was constructed. The return to reason and anti-religiosity which was emerging, especially in Europe, motivated a revaluation of the Greco-Roman cultures, resulting in a growth in representations from classical mythology in the arts of the period.

72 Maza, *La mitología . . .*, pp. 7-8.

Thus, the Iturbide Palace is not only a magnificent work of art but, also, a manifestation of the culture in New Spain in the eighteenth century, whose existence depends on the continued preservation of its historical memory.

The Palace of the Mayorazgo of the Canal Family

San Miguel de Allende, Guanajuato

The Palace of the Mayorazgo of the Canal Family

After having made a fabulous fortune in Mexico City, Don Manuel Francisco Tomás de la Canal y Bueno de Baeza, Knight of the Order of Calatrava, chose San Miguel el Grande (today San Miguel de Allende), a town inhabited by Spanish colonists, as the location in which to establish his residence and that of his heirs.

Gustavo Curiel

It is quite probable that the economic bonanza being enjoyed by the town during the eighteenth century encouraged him to undertake a series of varied business activities in the region, which proved very profitable. The imposing, palatial residence that his family constructed in San Miguel el Grande is a demonstration of the foregoing. Don Manuel de la Canal was baptized in the Parish Church of the Spanish, in Mexico City, on January 3, 1701. By 1732, he was already well established in the privileged city of San Miguel el Grande, in the Bajío region of Mexico, and had married Doña María Josefa Gabriela de Hervás y Flores, daughter of the wealthy miner, councilman and magistrate of Guanajuato, Don Juan de Hervás.[1] It should be pointed out that in Mexico City, the capital of the viceroyalty of New Spain, Don Manuel de la Canal had made an important demonstration of his generosity and artistic patronage, having paid for a *retablo*, or altarpiece, dedicated to St. Joseph, for one of the chapels of the Metropolitan Cathedral and had provided economic support to the Church of San Lorenzo.[2] With regard to his political career, it is noteworthy that he reached the post of councilman in Mexico City. According to the historian Miguel Malo Zozaya, the wealthy Creole also contributed to the sanctuaries of Guadalupe and La Piedad, in Mexico City.

Likewise, he sponsored the construction of two Santa Casas for Our Lady of Loreto, one in the church of the college of Jesuits, in Tepotzotlán, and the other for the Collegiate Church of San Gregorio, in Mexico City.[3] It should also be

1 Malo Zozaya, *La casa . . .*, pp. 38-39.

2 Ibid., p. 39.
With regard to the retablo that he commissioned for the cathedral, see: Maza, *San Miguel . . .*, (1939), p. 56.
With regard to the support provided to the Church of San Lorenzo, refer to the sixth clause of the document of the institution of the *mayorazgo*, in which is noted the amount of $3,000 pesos imposed on the hacienda San Joaquín de las Trancas. This can be found in Malo Zozaya, op. cit., p. 116.

3 Ibid.

mentioned here that, additionally, he contributed to the construction and decoration of the shrine to St. Joseph, a beautiful Baroque chapel of diminutive proportions annexed to the Santa Casa de Loreto of the church of the priests of the Society of Jesus, also in Tepotzotlán. The famed artist José de Ibarra included a portrait of him, as a donor, within the semicircular painting entitled *La huida a Egipto* (The Flight to Egypt).[4] It was in San Miguel el Grande, however, where this man and his wealthy family gave free reign to their patronage of the arts, as a result becoming great benefactors of this city of Spaniards. Worthy of note is the fact that Don Manuel paid the entire cost of the Santa Casa de Loreto, the chapel annexed to the Oratory Church of San Felipe Neri, in San Miguel el Grande, and promoted, although the project was never carried out, the construction of a convent for the Capuchin nuns adjacent to this church. According to Don Manuel's plan, the Santa Casa de Loreto was to serve, after its transformation, as a church for the nuns.[5] This notable Creole also provided the city with a system of baked-clay pipes and made improvements at the famous Del Chorro natural springs in order to supply the population with potable water.[6] He spent more than $200,000 pesos of his own money in improving the quality of life for the residents of the city via the construction of roads and other relevant public works.[7]

4 According to Francisco de la Maza, the oil painting is dated 1738. The portrait is of very good quality and has character. Don Manuel Francisco Tomás de la Canal was represented wearing a dark coat on the right side of which can be observed a Caravaca cross. This insignia is repeated on a piece of gold jewelry that hangs from his clothing. This benefactor holds a tricorn hat in his right hand. The accompanying inscription notes his role as a patron: "D. Manuel de la Canal, Knight of the Order of Calatrava and Councilman of Mexico City. Celebrated Benefactor of the Chapel."

5 "Autos de pedimento de el licenciado don Francisco Pérez de Espinosa, viceprefecto de el Oratorio de San Felipe Neri de la Villa de San Miguel el Grande, sobre el cumplimiento de una Real Cédula. 1738," Archivo General de la Nación, Mexico City. *Historia*, vol. 113. exp. 2-3, Fs. 101-201. The nuns that he planned to bring to San Miguel el Grande would have been Spanish Capuchins, subject to the rule of Santa Clara. Of note is that it is believed that José Mariano de la Canal paid for the construction of the Santa Casa de Loreto of the Santuario de Atotonilco, located near the city of San Miguel el Grande.

6 Barajas Becerra, *Apuntes . . .*, p. 121.

7 With regard to the economic power of this family, see: Sánchez de Tagle, "Una familia . . . ," pp. 115-124.

The Central Plaza of San Miguel el Grande

It is lamentable that sufficient information does not exist regarding the appearance of the central plaza in San Miguel el Grande prior to the seventeenth century. It can be noted, however, that this important space in the life of the population was laid out in a manner quite different from the current plaza. The old parish church, today the Chapel of San Rafael, also known as the Santa Escuela de Cristo, is oriented east to west, in contrast to the north-south orientation of the present-day parish church. The latter structure was built, by the architect Marcos Antonio Sobrarias, in the middle of the existing plaza.[8] Thus, it was during the seventeenth century when the central plaza of the city took on its present physiognomy. It is interesting to note, in terms of the subject matter presented within this text, that it is on the west side of this space where the magnificent palace of the Canal family was to be later built, in the eighteenth century.

Through the information to be found in *Vínculo del mayorazgo* (Entailment of the *Mayorazgo*) instituted by Don Felix de Berver y Vargas, on June 7, 1732, it is known that there were three private houses on the west side of the plaza:

8 The current Chapel of San Rafael, or Santa Escuela de Cristo, is actually the former parish church from the sixteenth century, transformed by Neo-Gothic elements that were added by Zeferino Gutiérrez (ca. 1901). This structure is the oldest church in San Miguel el Grande, built about 1578. Found in: Archivo General de la Nación, Mexico City, *Ordenanzas*, vol. 2, f. 220. In the atrium of this church, Marcos Antonio Sobrarias built the new church, about 1690-1698. The reader may refer to an interesting text by this architect regarding the condition of the existing church at the time and the construction of the new one, included in: Ramírez Montes, "La parroquia . . . ," pp. 97-106. It should be added that Sobrarias measured the original church as part of the preparation, noting that it was 51 varas long and 10.5 varas wide. These measurements coincide with the existing ones: 43.33 m x 8.97 m. Likewise, the architect mentions that the original church included two flying buttresses of recent construction, at the time, that is. These elements are still perceptible, located on the north wall of the church. It is the priest Agustín Morfi who clarifies the existence of two parish churches in the central plaza. In his famous work *Viaje de Indios y Diario del Nuevo México*, 1777-1778, he reports the following: "The central plaza is badly paved; one of its sides is occupied by the two parish churches, old and new; the other three are private houses, of no architecture and less magnificent."

the one to the north, whose owners at the time were the heirs of Nicolás de Solís, on the spot where some time later the stately palace of the Canal family was to be constructed, the one in the middle, the property of Don Felix de Berver y Vargas, and the one to the south, owned by Juan Serrano.[9] As with the majority of the public plazas in New Spain, around them were constructed the consistorial houses and the homes of the most important families in the given city. In the eighteenth century, this side of the plaza was home to the Canal, Muñoz Acosta and Sauto families. Something that speaks of the social relevance of the neighbors who shared the space surrounding the plaza is that all three of these families had founded *mayorazgos* (a contract established with the Crown by which the inheritance of the family's properties was guaranteed to the firstborn son). It should be added that on the east side of the plaza still stands the magnificent house which belonged to the Lanzagorta-Urtusuástegui family and, on the north side, that which pertained to Don Domingo de Aldama, a beautiful mansion also known as the Casa de la Conspiración (House of the Conspiracy).[10]

9 Fernández de Recas, *Mayorazgos . . .*, pp. 411-413.

10 The name Casa de la Conspiración is due to the fact that on the mezzanine level of the house, under the pretext of holding dances, political gatherings were held which contributed to the outbreak of the war for Independence. The most important families in the city were of Basque origin, principally from the towns of Gordejuela and Oquendo, near Vitoria, Spain. The Sauto, Jáuregui, Urtusuástegui and Allende families formed an important Basque group. With regard to the bitter conflict that developed between the Canal, Lanzagorta and Sauto families, involving business dealings, see: Salvucci, "Aspectos . . . ," pp. 405-443.

It is appropriate here to reproduce some of the text from the information provided by Don Felix de Berver y Vargas, elder clergyman of the bishopric of Michoacán, when he instituted his *mayorazgo*. In it, he states:

that because of how much I have and possess through my own two houses on the Public Plaza of this Town, the two-story ones, whose site [measures about 10 m across the front and 26 m deep]. Which borders said Public Plaza to the east, where said front lies; to the west with the houses of Don Francisco de Vargas, my brother; on the north with those of the heirs of Nicolás de Solís; and on the south with houses of Juan Serrano: Which existed and which I acquired by virtue of section and transfer, made mine by said Doña Antonia Muñoz de Acosta, my mother, in agreement of what was to fall to me and should be perceived as an inheritance from my legitimate mother, in writing in this Town [San Miguel el Grande]; its date, December 30, 1715.[11]

11 Fernández de Recas, loc. cit. See also: Archivo General de la Nación, Mexico City, *Vínculos y Mayorazgos*, vol. 15.

Everything seems to indicate that by 1732, the year in which Berver's *mayorazgo* was instituted, there already existed a public arcade on the west side of the plaza, or at least along part of it, in that in the foregoing documentation of the *mayorazgo*, the house and the one next to it, the service house, were noted as being of two stories. In order to construct houses above the public arcades along the plazas, it was necessary to obtain a special permit, via payment to the authorities of the city government, for such an exception to the zoning regulations. The construction of houses above the public arcades in the most important sites of such cities was undoubtedly an indication of social prestige.

Nevertheless, Don Manuel de la Canal was residing, with his wife, in a house situated on the outskirts of San Miguel el Grande at the time that he legally formed his own *mayorazgo*, on August 2, 1737. This property, which still exists today, was of great importance. The construction included

4.

a garden and orchard, a wall of stone and adobe [separating it from] the adjacent lot, which reaches [the house] to the north part, to the stream they call La Regadera, a vineyard that is opposite said house with 80,000 grapevines, its tank of stonemasonry, of [2.5 m deep, 16.8 m long and 13.4 m wide], with a dome of water fed by the city. The tract on which said vineyard lies, all of wheat land, of good quality, that [measures about 108 acres], fenced off on two sides, of stonemasonry, and a tannery immediately adjacent to the house mentioned.[12]

This enormous rural estate was appraised at the fabulous amount of $40,000 pesos, a true fortune at the time. Noteworthy is that that vineyard contained 80,000 grapevines. On the other hand, it is curious that among the clauses of the legal document regarding the foundation of the entailment of succession there is no reference to the family possessing another house in San Miguel el Grande, a surprising omission given the economic and social importance of the Canal-Hervás marriage. Within the information found in the document it is known that they also owned a house in the mining town of Santa Fe de Guanajuato.[13]

The wealth possessed by Don Manuel Francisco grew daily. Enormous revenues came in from two productive haciendas and various tracts of grazing land that he owned in the area. The hacienda San Joaquín de las Trancas, in the district corresponding to the city of San Miguel el Grande, was composed of thirteen large cattle pastures and three smaller ones. Subject to this hacienda were different "earthen barracks" on the farms San Nicolás and La Laborcilla. The other hacienda was Cuerámaro, in the district corresponding to the town of León. This hacienda included the grazing lands of Santa Cruz de Bañón and Nuestra Señora de Loreto, the latter purchased by Don Manuel from the Count de San Mateo de Valparaíso, who was an in-law. The rich hacienda Cuerámaro was composed of 130 large pastures and one and a half smaller ones.[14]

So that the reader may gain a clearer idea of the great number of animals pertaining to Don Manuel, in 1737, those that formed part of the *mayorazgo* are mentioned here. This also serves to explain the presence of the tannery adjacent to the house where he and his wife resided and their decisive participation in the production of San Miguel el Grande.[15]

Included in the *mayorazgo*, apart from the country estate, the two haciendas with their corresponding grazing land, etc., mentioned in the foregoing, were the following animals:

40,000	breeding ewes	50	colts
8,000	yearling sheep	100	branded colts
8,000	pairs of yearling sheep	700	mares on the hacienda Las Trancas
6,000	lambs	300	mares
200	horses	200	breeding mares
100	saddle mules	200	tame horses
30	draft mules, fitted		

12 See: Clause No. 22 of the document regarding the foundation of the *mayorazgo*, found in Malo Zozaya, op. cit. The house, although modified, is still conserved today. It now houses the Instituto Allende. The principal entrance is from a later period, perhaps from the same period as the construction on the house on the plaza in San Miguel el Grande. The same is true of the fountain in the courtyard. This structure is believed to have been destined, about 1809, as a convent for nuns of the Teresa order, a project by architect Manuel Tolsá which was never carried out. See: Maza, op. cit., pp. 98-100. Due to the quantity of water available from the La Regadera stream, the city's famous tanneries were situated in this area. Of interest is whether the Santa Elena tannery, which still exists, although greatly modified over the years, is the same one mentioned in the document regarding the foundation of the *mayorazgo*. Santa Elena is today (1999) a hotel.

13 See Clause No. 2 of the document regarding the foundation of the *mayorazgo*.

14 With regard to these properties, see Clause No. 22 of the document regarding the foundation of the *mayorazgo*.

15 As noted earlier, in the area around the country estate of the Canal family, today the Instituto Allende, the city's tanneries were located. Proof of this is a street named Tenerías (Tanneries) which is still named as such today.

100	saddle mules	200	colts
36	mules of six teams [of six] to pull the four-seat coaches	20	burros
		50	mules
		15	saddle mules
125	colts	100	tame oxen[16]

16 See the document regarding the foundation of the *mayorazgo*.

THE SUCCESSION OF THE MAYORAZGO

It is important to now to pause to take a look at the individuals who inherited the wealth of the *mayorazgo* instituted by the Canal-Hervás marriage. The first heir of the wealthy entailment was Don José Mariano Loreto de la Canal y Hervás, baptized on December 18, 1738. He died on April 20, 1794. Don José Mariano had married one of the daughters of the Count de Casa de Loja, Doña Mariana Francisca de Landeta de Primo. Everything was passed on, through the *mayorazgo* to their son, Don Narciso María Loreto José Juan Pedro Regalado de la Canal y de Landeta. He was baptized on November 4, 1758, and married his first cousin, Doña María Josefa de la Canal y de Landeta. When he died, on November 8, 1813, their son, Don Lorenzo María Loreto de Jesús José Joaquín Antonio Ignacio Tiburcio Juan Nepomuceno de la Canal y de Landeta inherited everything. He was baptized on August 11, 1798, and died on October 23, 1847.[17] Upon his death, after Mexico's independence from Spain, the institution of the *mayorazgo* had ceased to exist. It was inherited, only by title, by the Count de Samaniego. Of the heirs mentioned in the foregoing, most interesting is Don Narciso María Loreto de la Canal y de Landeta in that it seems that he was linked to the construction of the palace under study here.

17 The foregoing dates of baptism and death of these family members were taken from the genealogy of the Canal family prepared by Malo Zozaya (op. cit., pp. 47-99) and from Lámbarri de la Canal, *Prontuario* . . . . See the section dedicated to the Canal dynasty.

THE STYLISTIC AFFILIATION OF THE HOUSE AND THE POSSIBLE MODELS THAT INFLUENCED IT

The majority of historians who have written about the splendid palace in the Bajío region of Mexico coincide in affirming that it is a structure from the period of transition between the Baroque and the Neoclassical. Its construction has even been dated as occurring after 1800. It is necessary, however, to look more carefully at these judgments. Effectively, the building does contain a mixture of Baroque and Classical elements. As for the Baroque, we can observe the complicated spandrels of the colonnade on the east side of the house, the side facing the central plaza, in which the ornamentation includes representations of animals. Also there is the singular *rocaille* work (the product of an enlightened mind) that adorns the frames of the windows, the metopes of the friezes where the architect included thick motifs from this French repertoire, the complex ornamentation of the frieze and of the spandrels at the principal entrance, the rich and complex vegetal forms that inundate the interior of the scallop-shaped area of the niche which houses Our Lady of Loreto, as well as the spandrels of this vaulted niche, among other motifs. These elements can be easily classified as pertaining to Baroque patterns. There is also present in the house, however, in conjunction with the foregoing, cornices with dentils, monumental columns, pilasters of simple lines of the same colossal order, curved pediments and magnificent round openings integrated into the frames of the windows. These highly modern elements are from French Classicism, specifically the Louis XVI style, and not from the Neoclassical style being taught at the Academia de San Carlos, in Mexico City.

The historian Francisco de la Maza had made mention of the presence of motifs from the French Baroque in this house.[18] Likewise, some have seen in this palace the influence of the architectural models of the prestigious artists François Manzart and Louis Le Vau. What is certain is that the models by these notable architects could not have influenced the palace in question in that, apart from the Baroque details mentioned in the foregoing, it is of a decidedly Classical cut. The works by the aforementioned French artists date to the seventeenth century and their style has nothing to do with that executed on the Canal residence which obeys a later language, that of the Louis XVI style.

18 Maza, "Un paseo . . . ," p. 22. In this study, he states the following: "This palace was constructed by a grandson of Don Manuel Tomás, the Councilman and Royal Ensign Don Narciso Loreto de la Canal y Landeta, at the end of the eighteenth century. It is, without a doubt, one of the most beautiful residences in Mexico. Of Neoclassical style, although within it abound Baroque and Rococo elements. What greater sign of its Classical and anti-Baroque intentions than the Corinthian columns that that frame the entrance and the niche on the second floor? Additionally there are curved pediments, so favored by the Renaissance architects. The decoration of the spandrels and the frieze, of course, are from the French Baroque, but this merely indicates a richness incorporated into the initial plans, as with the coats of arms, that of the Casa Canal and that of the Casa Hervás."

In the mansion of the Canal family, the handling of three artistic languages is clear. One is derived from the Baroque variation native to New Spain, another is the French Classical (Louis XVI), and finally a style native to San Miguel el Grande itself. The last of these involves a formal repertoire which is present, primarily, in the singular manner in which the openings on the lower floor of the structure are framed, employing depressed arches, the same solution that appears in both the interior and exterior openings in this stately palace of rose-colored quarry stone, and reiterated in numerous civil constructions in the city, to such a degree that this type of enclosure of openings is distinctive of the area's civil architecture.

The architect, whose name remains unknown, was an artist with a taste for mixing various stylistic tendencies and architectural solutions, some of them of a notable modernity, with respect to the Baroque language of the final years of the eighteenth century.

Which of the Heirs of the Mayorazgo Ordered the Construction of the Residence?

Francisco de la Maza, and other writers who endlessly repeat what has been said by this researcher, have attributed the construction of the palace to Don Narciso María Loreto de la Canal y de Landeta, without any documental evidence. Considering the span of years in which this member of the family lived, his death occurring in 1813, it is quite probable that he had been the intellectual author of the building. But it is also possible that his father, Don José Mariano de Loreto de la Canal y de Hervás, who died on April 20, 1794, initiated the construction of the palace. Could this first heir of the *mayorazgo* have begun

the construction of the house and his son continued, based on the plans left by his father? Was the mansion constructed entirely during the lifetime of Don Narciso María Loreto? The answers to these questions will only be known if and when documents appear which can clarify such doubts and which can correctly attribute the construction to one or both of the family members mentioned. Israel Katzman has stated that it would not be farfetched to believe that the house had been completed by the end of the eighteenth century.[19] If this is true, the modernity of the Classical solutions to be found here are even more surprising. It is hoped that future research will define the dates as well as the name of the architect who constructed this magnificent house, doubtless one of the most important civil monuments in the entire Bajío region of Mexico.

19 Katzman, *Arquitectura . . .*, vol. I, p. 86.
In his work "Un paseo por San Miguel de Allende," Francisco de la Maza places the construction of this house during the final years of the eighteenth century. See Note 18.

The Louis XVI Models

As was noted earlier, the architect charged with the construction of this residence was an artist rather ahead of his time. He was familiar with the traditional Baroque forms in architecture as well as those derived from the Classicist models of the French from the eighteenth century. In order to understand, in its proper dimension, the decisive influence that was felt in the Americas from the Louis XVI models, one must consider the role played by engravings and architectural treatises in the transmission of the modern forms of this style. The former can explain the presence in this house of the formal dichotomy, the product of combined repertoires, opposing, from different periods, one Baroque and the other Classical. Essentially, the construction is exceedingly modern, one which the architect seems to have sprinkled with Baroque elements. If one observes the building carefully and, in an act of abstraction, eliminates the Baroque details from the spandrels, moldings, friezes, etc., he would be gazing upon a very modern palace with a Classicist cut. The palace of the Canal family is neither a finished nor a mature work, within the framework of academic art. How much of the conception of the building was influenced by the tastes of its owner? One must not lose sight of the fact that Don Narciso María Loreto was an enlightened human being. The residence is modern and avant-garde, the product of the Rationalist French influences of the period. It stands freed from the dictatorship of Reason.

Although it has already been noted that the name of the architect who built the house is unknown, the possibility should be pointed out that the project was carried out by an architect of renown and prestige from Mexico City. This is in line with the architectural skill, the modernity of the building for its time, the high quality of the work and the privileged status of the family that inhabited it. For the moment, it is impossible to attribute the work to a particular artist. The mansion is the product of an artist who, surely a well-experienced architect, also executed projects within the Neoclassical guidelines of the Academia de San Carlos. Figures such as José del Mazo y Avilés, Antonio González Velázquez,

Damián Ortiz de Castro, Miguel de Constanzó or Ignacio Castera are artists who participated in this dual tendency. It is worth considering that within this circle of artists, and their disciples, might be found the name of the architect of the palace of the Canal family.[20]

20 Antonio González Velázquez was in San Miguel el Grande to inspect the condition of the Church of the Concepción and had dealings with Don Narciso. José del Mazo y Avilés traveled to Guanajuato where he worked on the public granary in Granaditas.

It is necessary here to comment on some of the architectural and decorative elements of the palace in greater detail, those which clearly show the French Classicist influence, and point out certain concrete models and names of artists. For example, the singular use of round openings integrated into the windows-balconies of the mezzanine level and in the interior of the house have a great similarity to those executed by the architect Moreau-Desproux (1727-1793) on the ground floor of the Council of State of the Royal Palace in Paris.[21] In the works by this architect are also to be found similar openings, cornices with dentils, and curved pediments that are quite similar to those which appear on the palace in San Miguel el Grande. Of particular note is the pediment of the aforementioned Paris building which faces the Horology courtyard, as well as its cornices which divide the first floor from the second.

21 See: Planat.

Contant d'Ivry (1698-1777) participated, along with Moreau-Desproux, in the work on the Royal Palace in Paris. In fact, he later executed the magnificent façade of the Council of State building.[22] It should be noted that, within this Parisian work, the cornice of the second floor is broken in the identical manner as those which run along the exterior, as well as within the principal courtyard, of the home of the Canal family. Also of note is that the building in Paris includes individual sections of entablatures, placed along the columns, which are just like those of the palace in San Miguel el Grande.

22 Ibid.

The architect Louis executed a façade, between 1781 and 1786, on this same government building, that which faces the gardens of the Royal Palace in the City of Light. Within this prestigious work of Rationalist architecture can also be found formal similarities to those employed in the Canal house in San Miguel el Grande. In particular, one should note the enormous composite pilasters, the semicircular arches which feature richly ornamented spandrels, and the presence of individual cornices for each of the openings, which serve to separate the first and second levels of the façade.[23]

23 Ibid.

It is possible to believe that these architects, or other followers of the Louis XVI style such as Antoine, Soufflot, Gabriel Jacques-Ange, Patte, Richard Mique or De Wailly, provided the inspiration, through their work, for some of the formal solutions incorporated in the house of the Canal family.

Description of the Construction of the Building

The East Side

The structure of the side of the house which faces the central plaza is based on two levels which are perfectly differentiated,

accommodated on an irregular lot that presents a considerable slope on the west side. The lower level of the palace features a tall arcade composed of six open, semicircular arches. The keystones of these arches are enlivened by the presence of Baroque corbels ornamented with dense foliage. The extrados of the arches feature moldings including a thick listel which, along with the accompanying moldings produce a pleasant, Baroque play of light and shadow, typical of this style.

There are seven pilasters of the Doric order, placed on pedestals (lacking any ornamentation) and of monumental size in that they rise the entire height of the two levels of the residence. Their upper and lower extremes are finished with semicircular elements, those of the lower extremes featuring mixed lines while the upper ones are quite simple. These slim, graceful pilasters were also employed on the north façade and in the principal courtyard of the residence, areas which we will look at more closely further on.[24]

24 The monumental order employed in this house is the only example to be found in the city.

The colossal pilasters are connected by individual sections of architrave, aligned perfectly with the axes of these architectural elements. It is noteworthy that on the other faces of the house the architrave was eliminated, only the frieze and the cornice appearing, a notable anti-Classical solution born of the Baroque movement, which broke with the strict precepts of the Classical architecture of antiquity. The frieze is of the Doric order and is ornamented by alternating triglyphs and metopes. The triglyphs mark a successive one-three-one rhythm. In the area of the metopes, the architect chose to place motifs derived from the French *rocaille*, in the end creating an anti-Classical sensation of great novelty, far removed from academic art.

Finishing off the façade is the cornice which runs along the top. This is characterized by its molding which is recessed into the face. When hit by the rays of the sun, the forms of this cornice, with its recesses and projections of great dynamism, produce an intense play of light and shadow.

Six beautiful balconies open from the upper level and overlook the plaza. They are framed by depressed arches. For the spandrels created by these arches, the architect chose clusters of *rocaille* that hang over and to each side of the openings, disappearing in the areas between the balconies. At the base of the balcony openings are sections of cornice with moldings and dentils, one for each of the balconies. Above the area of the balconies are eaves, structured by an individual section of cornice, one for each opening. Curiously, the eaves are integrated into the openings by a bulbous section.[25]

25 These balconies were copied in the house of the Sauto family, situated along the same side of the central plaza.

The chromatic effect of this palace is surprising. Its construction employed a rose quarry stone of two tones, one darker than the other. The cornice, frieze, capitals, eaves, arches, spandrels, jambs and other important architectural elements were executed in stone of the darker tone, making it easy to appreciate the principal parts of the building. These elements seems suspended and stand out from the overall faces of the structure, which are of a softer tone. With these contrasting resources, the architect created a chromatic dynamism of great impact.

The balconies of the residence are of forged iron and can be catalogued, by their forms, as having been derived from the formal repertoire of Baroque art.

Casa del Cnel.
Simpatizador D
La Independencia
CANAL

In the upper part of the building, situated on either side of the individual sections of entablature described in the foregoing, which connect the Doric capitals of the monumental pilasters, are placed waterspouts. They were fabricated from quarry stone and include extensions of forged iron. The quarry-stone sections, it should be noted, were done in a square design. The length of the spouts allow that the runoff from the rainwater be directed onto the middle of the street rather than the sidewalk. The only spouts not found in pairs is that of the corner, which has a counterpart on the north side of the residence that fronts Canal street, formerly known as Real street.

The entire building, the exterior as well as the interior, follows an integral construction plan. It is apparent that the house was carefully thought out from the beginning and completed according to a master plan made before the construction began. There is no evidence of corrections or adjustments due to alterations or interruptions in the original plan.

The Arcade

The semicircular arches that form the structure of the arcade – certainly the only exterior arches of this type in terms of the city's civil architecture, with the exception of those of the public arcade on the west side of the plaza and those of the so-called Portal de Guadalupe, opposite the house – rest upon pilasters of the Doric order.[26] Supports of this type appear on each side of the monumental pilasters, structures into which they are imbedded. The pilasters are paneled and, curiously, have no bases and seem to rise from the ground. Not so in the case of the monumental pilasters which rest upon bases which are perfectly defined. Within the arcade are three groined arches, two of which delimit the house on its north and south ends and the third which is placed at the center of the arcade. The roof above this area is formed of closely spaced beams.

Within the arcade are eight openings on the building's wall with depressed arches, characteristic of the architecture in the region from the period of the viceroyalty. These openings provided access to the storefronts which once existed in the building, today adapted for use by the banking institution.

Of historical interest is that the most northerly of these spaces for many years housed the La Cucaracha cantina, an establishment of great tradition in San Miguel de Allende (as the city was renamed after Mexico's independence from Spain). Today, mariachi groups gather beneath the arcade of the house at night, waiting to be hired for a private serenade or to play in the central plaza. This has become their traditional meeting place. Another local tradition related to this arcade is that here one can purchase a variety of flowers that indigenous women offer for sale in the mornings, an activity that should be fostered lest it be lost.

In the northeast corner of the arcade is a flooring tile which bears the date 1895 (of quarry stone and popularly known as "San Miguelito," from the factory of the Sauto family). The inscription probably refers to improvements made to the paving. Interestingly, this is the only date which appears in the entire house.

26 Characteristic of the arches found in the Bajío is that they are not semicircular. The majority of the civil architecture is based on architraves or employs very depressed arches or those of short spans. As examples of the latter solution, one can observe the house of the *mayorazgo* of the Sauto family, at one time the Post Office and today unfortunately modified, which is situated on Correo street.

The Symbolic Program of the Palace

Within the decoration of the Canal mansion are two symbolic programs, specific and independent of each other. The first of these, and certainly quite simple, makes reference to the lineage of the Canal family, its social status and the reiterative devotion that the founder and the heirs of the *mayorazgo* professed for Our Lady of Loreto. In analyzing the principal entrance to the house, we will see each of these components. The second program was represented in the colonnades that form the east arcade of the house. Here, as well as inside the residence, the symbolism is simple.

On the spandrels of the arches there are to be found images of animals. There are fourteen in total, counting the two animals that were placed on the small section of the arcade which faces Canal street, formerly Real. On each of theses spandrels, the architect chose to place an animal. From left to right, on the first arch can be seen a pair of felines. On the second arch are two birds, which are perhaps quail. On the third arch can be distinguished a figure which might be a unicorn, and its corresponding animal, in this case, looks to be either a dog or a wolf. The fourth arch again features birds, to the left one with a large beak and, to the right, the image of either a duck or a goose. The fifth arch contains the image of a dog as well as one of a rabbit or hare. The spandrels of the sixth arch present the forms of what appear to be a porcupine or a wild boar and that of a bird. Finally, on the arch on the north face of this structure, which faces Canal street, there is to be found, on the left side, a long-necked bird. The image on the right side, however, has suffered damage and, therefore, cannot be identified. The symbolism carried by these figures is neither complicated nor very elaborated. They are merely representations of animals, of a decorative character. One must remember that representations of animals was a quite common decorative element in the civil architecture of San Miguel el Grande, as well as in Querétaro, during the period of the viceroyalty. The civil constructions in these two cities, which came to be known as houses of "Los Perros" (The Dogs), are examples of the foregoing.

The North Side of the House

The principal entrance, or "entrance of honor," is located on the north side of the construction, along what is, today, Canal street. In this part of the house, one can observe a considerable slope in the land, most noticeable on the west end of the parcel. This problem was ably resolved by the architect who constructed the residence. At the center of this part of the façade, the monumental entrance to the mansion was constructed. Of note is that on this side of the house there are three levels, or stories, which are perfectly differentiated on the exterior. The first of these was occupied by storefronts and the entrance to the service stairway, situated on the extreme west end. The second level pertains to the mezzanine of the residence while the third level is the area which was dedicated to the living quarters of the family. A constant in the civil architecture of New Spain, at least in terms of the homes of the wealthy, is that the rooms occupied by the families were always located on the upper floor of the houses. The storefronts and other spaces on the ground floor were rented to merchants or utilized as storage areas. The mezzanine had various uses. Sometimes it served as living quarters for a branch of the family of lesser economic means, or it was utilized to house offices or similar spaces related to the administration of the prosperous businesses of the owner of the house. The office of the owner himself, however, was generally located in a space on the ground floor and could be accessed from the vestibule, such was the case in this house. The spaces on the upper floor, as just mentioned, were the rooms in which the owner and his family passed their time, entertained guests and where the private chapel, the drawing room, the living areas, bedrooms, etc., were located.

The architect employed three solutions for the openings on the north side of the residence, a different one for each of the three levels of the house. On the ground floor there are depressed arches which rest on jambs with moldings that directly connect and interrelate them without marking or making apparent the union of both constructive elements, a solution characteristic of the civil architecture of San Miguel el Grande. For the mezzanine level, balconies were introduced into whose frames were integrated magnificent circular openings with chamfered edges. In the area above the round openings can be observed a small corbel formed of vegetal elements. Eight of these balconies are distributed along the building's face at the mezzanine level. On the top floor, the solution employed for the balconies at this same level on the east façade is repeated. There are a total of eight balconies and the frames and spandrels are ornamented with a *rocaille* motif. The differentiation of the two levels through these varying solutions grants the building an orderly character which is, at the same time, also dynamic.

Just as with the façade that faces the central plaza, the architect again employed monumental pilasters, this time seven and identical to those previously described. The east end of this side, which we have already analyzed, forms part of the arcade and has the same features as the part which fronts the plaza. The upper extremes of the colossal pilasters, of the Doric order, are treated in the same manner as their counterparts on the east façade. These supports are connected by an individual section of entablature. Immediately above the entablature can be observed a section of triglyphs and the cornice which runs along the axes of the pilasters. These architectural solutions grant the house great movement with regard to the uppermost part of the building.

The Principal Entrance

The magnificent and monumental entrance features, in its first volume, two columns, nearly disengaged, which are fluted along the lower third of the shafts. The gigantic supports appear crowned with capitals of the Corinthian order. The opening of the entrance, it should be noted, is similar

in form to that utilized in the framing of the storefront openings along the ground floor of the building, only larger, in accordance with the enormous proportions of the entrance. On the keystone of the entrance arch is placed a carving, in high relief, featuring an eagle. This bird is seen biting into a serpent which would seem to indicate that it represents the symbol associated with the founding of the indigenous city which today is Mexico City.[27] It is possible that the inclusion of this symbol at the entrance is an allusion to the fact that Don Manuel de la Canal, the founder of the dynasty, had been born in Mexico City. The spandrels of the entrance contain exuberant vegetal motifs that seem influenced by the voluptuous rhythms that animate the eighteenth-century French *rocaille*. The architrave, on the contrary, is smooth and presents no ornamentation whatsoever. Not so with the frieze, however, an element on which not a square inch of space was left without ornamentation. The decoration of this architectural element is affiliated, artistically, to that which appears on the spandrels of the entrance arch.

27 The figure of the serpent is difficult to make out, indicating that part of this figure may have been lost over time.

Aligned with the axes formed by the enormous Corinthian columns can be appreciated a pair of individual sections of cornice. One characteristic of the supports is that they stick out a bit from the face of the building. The first volume of the entrance is crowned by an enormous yet graceful curved pediment, decorated on the inside and at the bottom with a series of dentils. Within the tympanum was placed a bas-relief whose carving was never completed. As such, it remains little more than a sketch.[28]

28 Given that the relief remains without detailing, it has been impossible to infer the motif chosen to decorate this part of the pediment.

Attention is called immediately by the splendid Baroque door, of wood, which closes off the entrance opening of the house. Its decoration is exuberant. There are four valances formed from irregular lines, placed in pairs at the top and bottom of each of the two leaves of the door. The upper valances are larger than those at the bottom. These ornamental elements express an imbalance in the order (a solution unique to Baroque) and grant great movement to the door. The edges of the door are serpentine, just as are the lengths of cornice placed in the middle of the lower part and in the finishing of the upper valences. The artistic conception of the door contrasts greatly with the simple lines of the framing elements around it and the smooth shafts of the monumental columns that frame it.

The second volume of the entrance is an area into which a niche was integrated. Pairs of Doric columns, of the same style as those of the part beneath, but of lesser size, frame the niche. Within it is found the image of the protector of the *mayorazgo*, Our Lady of Loreto. This Marian sculpture, of excellent artistic quality, is placed above a naive representation of a house. A representation of clouds is visible between the ceiling of the niche and sculpted image. The Virgin is accompanied by the Christ Child and lacks, as is typical of this type of representation of her, both hands and arms. As such, there is an allusion to the moment of the miraculous transference of the house of Mary, from Nazareth to Loreto, Italy. A splendid crown of forged iron encircles the head of the Virgin. The grooves on the interior of the niche, framed by a semicircular arch, present ornamentation that recalls the grooves of a scallop shell. The hinge of the scallop shell seems to have been eliminated. The spandrels around the niche also feature decoration derived from

Banamex

the French *rocaille*. Atop the four capitals of the columns are located moldings which are similar to sections of architrave, which are connected to cubes and, as such, achieve even greater height. In turn, these elements serve to support a curved pediment with dentils on which is placed, on the upper middle part, the representation of a cross, a distinctive symbol of the prestigious Order of Calatrava. One will remember that Don Manuel Francisco Tomás de la Canal became a member of this military order in 1731.[29] The heirs of the *mayorazgo* were also Knights of Calatrava and royal ensigns of the city of San Miguel el Grande.

One section of the cornice projects beyond the axis of the space in which the entrance is placed. It is important to note that the axes which are formed by the monumental columns of the first volume of the entrance were topped, above the larger pediment, by two noble coats of arms. These symbols represent the two families whose marriage gave birth to the *mayorazgo*. To the left is the one which corresponds to the surname Canal while to the right is that of the Hervás family. In turn, both coats of arms are topped by helmets with feathered crests.[30] Fortunately, these representations were not erased when an independent Mexico destroyed the coats of arms of the nobility as well as any other iconography allusive to the Spanish on public buildings and private homes.

In summary, apart from the symbols of family (coats of arms) and of social status (the cross of Calatrava) there is also present at the entrance the protector of the family (Our Lady of Loreto) and a bird which alludes, possibly, to the birthplace of the father of the Canal dynasty in the Americas, Mexico City.

The Interior of the House

The Vestibule

This was an important space in the civil constructions from the period of the viceroyalty. The vestibule was the point of transition between the interior of the house and the street. From this point, the service staff would direct visitors to the house to other spaces, according to their hierarchy and interests. In the vestibule, messages could be left for the owner, and here the firewood, coal, etc., was paid for and temporarily deposited. Upon entering from the street, to the right was located the entrance to the office, or study, of the Canal family. Here the books were kept regarding the haciendas, the ranches, the grazing lands and the other properties and activities linked to the *mayorazgo*. Surely, it was also here were the employees of the workshops and tanneries would come to receive their pay.

The wall of the vestibule opposite the street entrance is marked by a simple doorway of quarry stone, composed of pilasters that support a semicircular arch made up of wedge-shaped stones. Through it, one gained access to the principal courtyard of the house.

29 Malo Zozaya, op. cit., p. 38.

30 The coat of arms of the Canal family has been described in the following manner: "In the foreground, against a field of gules, a stone castle with three towers, with four flags, and atop the central tower a man armed with another flag in his hand. In the upper left corner a golden castle. In the background, an azure sinister, a simple cross of gules, quartered in the center by two stars of eight radii, and in the lower left corner a fleur-de-lis; half a shield of azure with a stone bridge of a single span. Curved lines of water of azure and silver. As a crest for the shield the cross of the military order of Calatrava." Malo Zozaya, op. cit., pp. 27-28.

The Principal Courtyard or Courtyard of Honor

The mansion of the Canal family contained two courtyards, the principal and the service courtyard. The first of these, due to its importance and significance within the dynamics of the house, is richly ornamented and its monumental pilasters are notable. The architectural solution is based on a square plan and two levels, perfectly differentiated. The north and south sides of the courtyard are similar in structure and decoration. Within the courtyard are three colonnades, on both the ground and top floors, composed of semicircular arches, which form corresponding arcades. The east side of the courtyard features one of these arcades, on the upper floor, while its ground floor counterpart, as well as the west side are closed off. The arches feature molding and present a corbel which functions as the keystone of each of them. They are similar to the arches which form the arcade that faces the plaza. Of great importance are the monumental pilasters which structure the space, two on each side except for the west side, which has only one. Apart from these supports, the architect placed a pilaster in each of the four corners whose characteristics include their being sectioned in quarter round. This novel and audacious solution that the architect employed in the structuring of the corners becomes an interesting interplay of mixed lines evident, principally, in the thick cornice that crowns and enlivens the courtyard at the upper level. In this manner, the architect eliminated the arrises at the corners. The seven other pilasters are identical to those of the exterior of the building, their capitals connected to individual sections of entablature. Here we notice a frieze which includes corbels distributed in the manner of triglyphs, which terminates at the top with individual cornices of straight lines that project with respect to the principal plan of the building. These thick sections of cornice contrast with the mixed lines which finish off the corner pilasters. The two floors of the house are separated by the presence of sections of cornice with dentils, sometimes individual sections, such as those on the north, east and south sides, or continuous, as is the case on the west side. On the upper part of the wall on the east side, noteworthy is the presence of three circular openings, with moldings chamfered toward the interior. A single such opening is repeated on the west wall. In this same area is another opening but of mixed lines, characteristic of the Baroque language. Its presence permits the illumination of the principal staircase of the house.

Another aspect of the ornamentation of the palace that is worth noting is the presence of panels which contain *rocaille* ornamentation. These are placed between the arches and the sections with dentils. These ornamental forms are also present in the triglyphs of the frieze. The *rocaille* panels are magnificently executed.

Next we turn to the Doric pilasters, above which are placed the semicircular arches which form the arcades. A principal characteristic of these is that they are imbedded in the monumental pilasters. Their ornamentation features panels placed in three sections along their lengths, a solution that is also present in the intrados of the arches. The spandrels of the arcades of the upper floor are filled with *rocaille* forms that enliven the areas. The waterspouts, identical to those

on the exterior of the mansion, are placed on either side of the monumental pilasters. In the corners there is one spout each, placed above the architrave of the quarter round pilasters. Their rhythm is two-two-one.

Crossing the threshold of the vestibule, along the north arcade, one finds the principal staircase that leads to the mezzanine and on to the upper floor of the residence. There is not the slightest doubt that this mezzanine was the most notable in the city. The modest mezzanine found in the house which once belonged to Don Domingo de Aldama, on Relox street, cannot compare in terms of the size and the ornamentation of this one. The mezzanine of the house of the Canal family is large and its rich decoration on the exterior grants it relevance. Upon considering a space with such characteristics within this house, one begins to see the influence, in this provincial building, of the palatial mansions constructed in Mexico City.

The principal rooms of the mezzanine level on the north side of the house feature ceilings of tightly spaced beams which were painted with rich decorations based on geometric motifs, quite possibly a product of the nineteenth century. The window-balconies open to the outside and allow for ventilation and adequate illumination. The doorways leading into the rooms on the mezzanine are composed of depressed arches which rest on jambs with moldings, similar to those described on the ground floor of the building.

The principal staircase is of a single access and includes, on the second flight, a handrail of quarry stone. At the top of the staircase are two openings. One of them is the access to the rooms on the upper floor while the second houses a surprising stand for placing earthenware water containers. This served the original inhabitants in that they had access to water at any hour of the day or night. It is adorned by a frame of carved stone that includes *rocaille* ornamentation on the lower part. From this frame hangs a valance which contains, at the center, a grotesque, created from vegetal forms, which spews out dense foliage. A wooden grille covers the front of this space, and it is noteworthy that it is located in the coolest area of the house, the north side.

The Private Chapel

The most important wing of the upper floor is that on the west side of the courtyard where, originally, the drawing room, the private chapel and another, small room were to be found. It is possible that this small room was intended to be used to place a portrait of the Spanish monarch beneath a canopy.[31] A pictorial program can be observed on the walls of these rooms, composed, principally, of motifs from the French *rocaille*. Some of the sections of the pictorial program have been retouched while others have been left without restoration as witnesses to their original character. In photographs from the period, another pictorial program, no longer existing, can be observed, a product of the nineteenth century that covered the walls in this area of the house.

Just before reaching the anteroom, which is parallel to the drawing room, lies the entrance to the private chapel of the Canal family. It is composed of a

31 Such special rooms were the privilege of those who had obtained titles from the crown. Don Narciso María Loreto de la Canal was negotiating such a title when the war for independence from Spain broke out. See: Malo Zozaya, op. cit., pp. 24-25. It is possible that this small room, situated next to the drawing room, had been contemplated for such use.

semicircular arch sustained by pilasters and flanked by fluted columns crowned with Doric capitals. Above these elements is an entablature with an architrave which features moldings. The frieze includes, at the center, the figure of a cherub. The cornice is double and contains dentils. A pair of volutes, of thick lines, curl inward and create an area which houses an ornate relief that includes a representation of the Annunciation. On each volute is an inscription: the one on the left is *Electa ut Sol* and on the right is *Pulchra ut Luna*, phrases allusive to the purity of the Virgin Mary. The relief at the center is of a Baroque conception. A drapery is held open to reveal the moment when the archangel Gabriel announces to Mary that she is to be the Mother of the Savior. The axes marked by the columns, nearly disengaged, are finished off with small cubes placed above the cornice. The spandrels of the arch are completely filled with complex and exuberant motifs derived from the French *rocaille*. The Baroque wooden door to the chapel is paneled, was richly carved and includes representations of the Tower of David and the Well of Grace. These symbolic elements were taken from the Litany of Loreto and indicate to the spectator that the chapel was dedicated to a Marian, in this case Our Lady of Loreto.

The entire entrance is polychromatic, parts of it resembling marble, with golden details on the capitals, the spandrels, the frieze, the top of the cornice and the volutes. Outside the portal can be observed a painted border which delimits it.

The interior of the chapel of this powerful family conserved, for many years, a painting of Our Lady of Loreto, protector of the family, as has already been mentioned.

In the information found in the document related to the institution of the *mayorazgo*, there is mention of this painting and, curiously, this portrait also formed part of the legal entailment:

[A] superior image of Our Lady of Loreto, of [about 60 centimeters square], more or less, painted in fine clothing, in half-length, brown color, blue background, with silver stars, and its title along the edge, which says 'Vera effigies Beatissime virginis Marie Lauretane'; influenced by the original which is venerated in her Holy House in Nazareth, [in the district of] Ancona; a copy faithful to the original, which has captured the primary attention of our humble devotion and reverence; for which its greatest worship has been procured, having it in the principal salon of our house, with the light of day and of night. And in the same manner it is our will and the express Condition of this Entailment and Mayorazgo, *that our successors, possessors of it, have this superior image and under no circumstances in the aforementioned house . . . and we want that it remain in our house the expressed [painting] that we leave entailed. And we declare, so that our successors so practice, having had customs all the years that [it] go in the month of July to the Holy House referred to, and that it stay there nine days with their nights; say another number of masses, the first and last sung, with the litany, maintaining without*

intermission two candles lit of fine wax, de tres en libra, *which we want executed by all the possessors of this* mayorazgo.[32]

32 Ibid., pp. 109-110. Although the image was, according to this information documented in the *mayorazgo* documents, in the house on the outskirts of the city, it must have been moved to the house on the plaza, for the importance and the devotion it held for the family.

The Service Courtyard

Although smaller and of less ornamention than the principal courtyard, the service courtyard is of surprising beauty. Outstanding is the simplicity and purity of its structural lines. The diverse spaces adjacent to it were distributed along three of its sides: the north, east and west. There were no rooms on the south side, which is comprised of a high wall which marks the boundary of the lot and is finished with a single, inverted arch whose characteristic is that of being depressed. There are arcades only on the north and east sides. The spaces feature beamed ceilings like those of the rest of the house.

In this courtyard were concentrated the different facilities for the maintenance and service of the residence, such as the kitchen, the manger, the foodstuffs, storerooms, etc.

The arches of the arcades are semicircular and rest on pilasters of different heights, according to the importance of the floor on which they are found. Those of the upper floor are of greater height. The mezzanine level of this courtyard is perfectly differentiated from the rest of the structure.

On the upper floor there is a panel of considerable dimensions, located on the north wall, where a landscape was painted. The advanced degree of deterioration does not allow for the proper determination of the theme represented. Everything seems to indicate that it has to do with a country scene, quite naive, surely a product of the nineteenth century. Some of the other houses in this city also conserve painted murals, of similar characteristics, in the arcades of their courtyards.

In the northeast corner of the upper floor of the residence is a water tank. It is quadrangular in shape and the bottom of the receptacle is covered by glazed ceramic tiles of complex designs, perhaps fabricated in the town of Dolores. The tile work is very similar to that which covers the floor of the niche which houses Our Lady of Loreto of the Oratory (a work also sponsored by this same family). It should be noted that Dolores was, and still is, a town known for the production of enameled ceramics. The water tank allowed the servants of the house easy access to water for use on the upper floor of the mansion. From here, the water necessary for the kitchen was drawn, as well as that required for watering the plants which lined the arcades during the period. It should be pointed out that another stand for accommodating water jugs exists, situated along the north wall of the ground floor of the house. It is small in comparison to the one located at the top of the principal staircase, described earlier. It must be assumed that this smaller one, in the service courtyard, was used by the household staff and other servants.

The rooms along the west side served to house the animals and as storerooms. Also located here were the four-seater coaches and the grander carriages of the members of this powerful family.

There is a service staircase located in this courtyard and, curiously, there is an independent entrance on Canal street. Via this entrance, the servants utilized this staircase to move between the ground floor, the mezzanine, the upper floor and the roof, without having to use the principal staircase.

A Distinguished Guest

When the last of the Canal family left the palace, in the nineteenth century, the house was adapted for use as the Hotel Allende. In 1873, the famous singer Ángela Peralta was a guest of the hotel. The diva, popularly known as the "Mexican Nightingale," interpreted before the public of San Miguel de Allende such works and Rigoletto,. Ruy Blas, Il Trovatore and Lucia de Lammermoor.[33] The city of San Miguel de Allende, in recognition of the visit made by the famous diva, renamed the public theater in her honor. During her stay at the hotel, Peralta no doubt stepped onto one of the balconies of this palace in order to greet the multitude of admirers who wished to meet her or at least see her.

33 Maza, *San Miguel . . .*, (1972), p. 133. I wish to thank musicologist Clara Meierovich for her commentary on the programs of the performances of this singer.

After a period as a hotel, the house of the Canal family became, once again, a private home, this time for the family of Don Albino García. Still famous today are the balls held in the house by Armando García in the 1930s. This family sold the building to Banco Nacional de México, in 1981. The banking institution immediately began a restoration project. The work was entrusted to architect Juan Cortina del Valle and lasted until 1985. A second intervention on the part of the bank was carried out by architects Ramiro Alatorre and Carlos Villela between 1997 and 1998.

General Bibliography

Abundis Canales, Jaime and Juan Antonio Siller C. "La casa del Adelantado Francisco Montejo en Mérida." *Cuadernos de arquitectura virreinal* 1, (1985), pp. 25-45.

Alamán, Lucas. *Historia de México*, Mexico City: Lara, 1849-1852.

Alberro, Solange. *Del gachupín al criollo*. Mexico City: El Colegio de México, 1992.

Almonte, Juan Nepomuceno. *Guía de forasteros de México y repertorio de conocimientos útiles.* Mexico City: Imprenta de I. Cumplido, 1852.

Ancona, Eligio. *Historia de Yucatán desde la época más remota hasta nuestros días.* 2d ed. Barcelona: Imprenta de Jaime Jesús Roviralta, 1889.

Angulo Iñiguez, Diego, et al. *Historia del arte hispano-americano.* 3 vols. Mexico City: Salvat Editores, 1945-1950.

______. *Historia del arte hispano-americano.* Mexico City: Instituto de Investigaciones Estéticas y Documentos Históricos, Universidad Nacional Autónoma de México, 1982.

Argan, Giulio Carlo. *Historia del arte como historia de la ciudad.* Barcelona: LAIA, 1983.

Barajas Becerra, Antonio. *Apuntes para la historia de la ciudad de San Miguel de Allende, 1542-1992.* Querétaro: Formas Administrativas, 1992.

Bargellini, Clara. *La arquitectura de la plata: iglesias monumentales del centro-norte de México, 1640-1750.* Madrid: Turner / Universidad Nacional Autónoma de México, 1991.

______, et al. *Historia y arte en un pueblo rural norteño: San Bartolomé, ahora Valle de Allende, Chihuahua.* Mexico City: Universidad Nacional Autónoma de México, 1998.

Bartra, Roger. *El salvaje en el espejo.* [traslation] Mexico City: Editorial Era / Universidad Nacional Autónoma de México / Coordinación de Difusión Cultural, 1992.

Bérchez, Joaquín. "Arquitectura mexicana de los siglos XVII y XVIII." *Arte novohispano* 3 (1992).

Berlanga Fernández de Córdoba Moncada, Guillermo. "El palacio de Moncada y los mayorazgos del Jaral de Berrio y de San Mateo de Valparaíso." *El palacio de Iturbide.* Mexico City: Fomento Cultural Banamex, 1972.

______, et al. *El palacio de Iturbide.* Mexico City: Fomento Cultural Banamex, 1972.

Berlin, Heinrich. "Three master architects in New Spain." *The Hispanic American Historical Review*, vol. XXVII, no. 2, (1947), p. 381.

Berrojalbiz, Fernando y Miguel Vallebueno. "Grupos vascos en la región de Durango. Joseph del Campo Soberrón y Larrea, conde del Valle del Súchil." Vol. I of *Los vascos en las regiones de México.* Mexico City: Universidad Nacional Autónoma de México / Ministerio de Cultura del Gobierno Vasco, 1996, pp. 246-263.

Bustos, Gerardo. *Libro de las descripciones sobre la visión geográfica de Yucatán en textos españoles del Siglo XVI.* Mexico City: Universidad Nacional Autónoma de México, 1988.

Calderón de la Barca, Madame. *Life in Mexico. During a Residence of Two Years in that Country.* New York: E. P. Dutton and Co. Inc., 1931.

Castro Morales, Efraín. "Los maestros mayores de la Catedral de México." *Artes de México*, año XXI, núms. 182-183 (1976), p. 143.

Catálogo Nacional de Monumentos Históricos Inmuebles, Centro Histórico (Perímetro A). coor. Eugenia Prieto Inzunza. 3 vols. Mexico City: Departamento del Distrito Federal / Consejo del Centro Histórico / Secretaría de Educación Pública / Dirección de Monumentos Históricos, Instituto Nacional de Antropología e Historia, 1988.

Cervantes de Salazar, Francisco. *México en 1554.* ed. Edmundo O'Gorman, Sepan Cuantos . . . . 25. 6th ed. México City: Editorial Porrúa, 1985.

Chamberlain, Robert S. *Conquista y colonización de Yucatán, 1517-1550.* Mexico City: Editorial Porrúa, 1974.

Chávez, Samuel. *El Arte y la Ciencia. Revista mensual de Bellas Artes e Ingeniería.* vol. I, núm. 1 (1899), pp. 4-6.

Estrada de Gerlero, Elena. "El tesoro perdido de la catedral michoacana." *La Catedral de Morelia.* Mexico City: El Colegio de Michoacán / Gobierno del Estado de Michoacán, 1992.

Fernández de Recas, Guillermo S. *Mayorazgos de la Nueva España.* Mexico City: Universidad Nacional Autónoma de México / Biblioteca Nacional de México / Instituto Bibliográfico Mexicano, 1965.

Palace of the Count de San Mateo de Valparaíso. Mexico City.

Fernández, Justino. *El palacio de Minería.* 2d ed. Mexico City: Instituto de Investigaciones Estéticas, Universidad Nacional Autónoma de México, 1985.

Fernández, Martha. "El 'neóstilo' y las primeras manifestaciones de la Ilustración en Nueva España." *Anales del Instituto de Investigaciones Estéticas* 64. Universidad Nacional Autónoma de México (1993).

Flores Marini, Carlos. "El Palacio de Iturbide. Antecedentes artísticos." *El palacio de Iturbide.* Mexico City: Fomento Cultural Banamex, 1972.

Gallegos, Juan Ignacio. *Historia de Durango 1563-1910.* Gómez Palacio, Durango: Impresiones Gráficas México, 1984.

Gante, Pablo C. de. *La arquitectura de México en el siglo XVI.* Mexico City: Talleres Gráficos de la Nación, 1947.

García Ávila, Sergio. "El crédito y las instituciones financieras 1880-1910." Vol. III of *Historia general de Michoacán.* Mexico City: Instituto Michoacano de Cultura, 1989.

García Bernal, Manuela Cristina. *Población y economienda en Yucatán bajo los Austrias.* Seville: Escuela de Estudios Hispanoamericanos de Sevilla, 1978.

Gerhard, Peter. *The North Frontier of New Spain.* Princeton: Princeton University Press, 1982.

Gómiz, Everardo. *Monografía de Nombre de Dios, Poanas y Súchil.* 2d ed. Durango: 1980.

Gonzalbo Aispuru, Pilar. *Las mujeres en la Nueva España.* Mexico City: El Colegio de México, 1987.

González Franco, Glorinela, et al. "Notas para una guía de artistas y artesanos de la Nueva España II." *Boletín Monumentos Históricos* 4. Instituto Nacional de Antropología e Historia (1980).

González Galván, Manuel. *Arte virreinal en Michoacán.* Mexico City: Frente de Afirmación Hispanista, 1978.

González-Polo, Ignacio, et al. *Edificaciones del Banco Nacional de México. Seis virreinales y una contemporánea.* Mexico City: Fomento Cultural Banamex, 1988.

______. "El arquitecto Francisco Antonio Guerrero y Torres." *El palacio de Iturbide.* Mexico City: Fomento Cultural Banamex, 1972.

______. "Memorial relativo al llamado Palacio de Iturbide." *Anales del Instituto Nacional de Antropología e Historia.* 7ª época, tomo 3, años 1970-1971 (1973), pp. 79-96.

______. "El palacio de los condes de Santiago de Calimaya." *Cuadernos de historia del arte* 2. Instituto de Investigaciones Estéticas, Universidad Nacional Autónoma de México, 1973.

______. "Los palacios señoriales del marqués del Jaral construidos por Guerrero y Torres en la ciudad de México." *Edificaciones del Banco Nacional de México. Seis virreinales y una contemporánea.* Mexico City: Fomento Cultural Banamex, 1988.

Grimal, Pierre. *Diccionario de mitología griega y romana.* 5th printing. Barcelona: Paidós, 1991.

______, et al. Vol I of *Mitologías del Mediterráneo al Ganges.* Barcelona: Editorial Planeta, 1973.

Guijo, Gregorio Martín. Vol II of *Diario, 1648-1664.* ed. Manuel Romero de Terreros. Mexico City: Editorial Porrúa, 1953.

Gurría Lacroix, Jorge. "Biografía del antiguo palacio de Moncada." *El palacio de Iturbide.* Mexico City: Fomento Cultural Banamex, 1972.

Hernández, Carlos. *Durango gráfico.* Durango: 1903.

Herrejón Peredo, Carlos. *Los orígenes de Guayangareo-Valladolid.* Mexico City: El Colegio de Michoacán / Gobierno del Estado de Michoacán, 1991.

Ibarrola Arriaga, Gabriel. *Familias y casas de la vieja Valladolid.* Morelia: Fimax Publicistas, 1969.

Jaramillo, Juvenal. *La vida académica de Valladolid en la segunda mitad del siglo XVIII.* Morelia: Universidad Michoacana de San Nicolás de Hidalgo, 1989.

Juárez Nieto, Carlos. *El clero en Morelia durante el siglo XVII.* Mexico City: Instituto Michoacano de Cultura / Centro Regional Michoacán del Instituto Nacional de Antropología e Historia, 1988.

Katzman, Israel. Vol. I of *Arquitectura del siglo XIX en México.* Mexico City: Centro de Investigaciones Arquitectónicas, Universidad Nacional Autónoma de México, 1973.

Kubler, George. *Arquitectura mexicana del siglo XVI.* Mexico City: Fondo de Cultura Económica, 1982.

Ladd, Doris M. *La nobleza mexicana en la época de la Independencia, 1780-1826.* Mexico City: Fondo de Cultura Económica, 1984.

Lafora, Nicolás. *Relación del viaje que hizo a los presidios internos, situados en la frontera de la América septentrional perteneciente al rey de España.* ed. Vito Alessio Robles. Mexico City: Robredo, 1939.

Lámbarti de la Canal, Roberto. *Prontuario de familias que tuvieron renombre o fortuna en San Miguel el Grande durante los siglos XVIII y XIX.* Mexico City: unpublished, 1986.

Landa, Diego de. *Relación de las cosas de Yucatán.* Mérida: Producción Editorial Dante, 1986.

Legorreta, Agustín. "Prólogo." *El palacio de Iturbide.* Mexico City: Fomento Cultural Banamex, 1972.

Legorreta, Ricardo. "Criterio arquitectónico en la restauración del Palacio de Iturbide." *El palacio de Iturbide.* Mexico City: Fomento Cultural Banamex, 1972.

Lemoine, Ernesto. "Documentos para la historia de Valladolid, hoy Morelia, 1541-1642." *Boletín del Archivo General de la Nación.* 2ª época, tomo III, núm. 1, (1962).

López de Cogolludo, Diego. *Los primeros vecinos de la Ciudad de Mérida.* Mérida: Impresora Oriente, 1935.

______. *Historia de Yucatán,* Colección de Grandes Crónicas Mexicanas. México City: Editorial Academia Literaria, 1957.

Luca de Tena, Torcuato. *Ciudad de México en tiempos de Maximiliano.* 2d reprinting. Mexico City: Planeta, 1990.

Malo Zozaya, Miguel J. *La casa y mayorazgo de la Canal de la Villa de San Miguel el Grande (Nueva España).* Mexico City: private edition, undated.

Manrique, Jorge Alberto. "El 'neóstilo': la última carta del barroco mexicano." *Historia Mexicana* 79 (enero-marzo 1971), pp. 335-367.

Marroqui, José María. *La ciudad de México.* 3 vols. Mexico City: J. Aguilar Vera y Cía, 1900-1903.

Maza, Francisco de la. *La ciudad de Durango, notas de arte.* Mexico City: Imprenta Gama, 1948.

______. "Un paseo por San Miguel de Allende." *Artes de México* 139. año XVIII, undated.

______. *San Miguel de Allende, su historia, sus monumentos.* Mexico City: Instituto de Investigaciones Estéticas, Universidad Nacional Autónoma de México, 1939.

______. *La mitología clásica en el arte virreinal de México.* Estudios y Fuentes del Arte en México 24. Mexico City: Instituto de Investigaciones Estéticas, Universidad Nacional Autónoma de México, 1968.

______. *El arte colonial en San Luis Potosí.* Mexico City: Universidad Nacional Autónoma de México, 1969.

______. *San Miguel de Allende. Su historia. Sus monumentos.* Mexico City: Frente de Afirmación Hispanista, A.C., 1972.

Mazín, Oscar. *El Gran Michoacán.* Mexico City: El Colegio de Michoacán / Gobierno del Estado de Michoacán, 1986.

______. "Presentación." *Archivo Capitular de Administración Diocesana Valladolid-Morelia. Catálogo I.* Mexico City: El Colegio de Michoacán / Gobierno del Estado de Michoacán, 1991.

______. "La catedral de Valladolid y su cabildo eclesiástico." *La Catedral de Morelia.* Mexico City: El Colegio de Michoacán / Gobierno del Estado de Michoacán, 1992.

______. *El Cabildo de la Catedral de Valladolid de Michoacán,* Mexico City: El Colegio de Michoacán, 1996.

Medina Rubio, Arístides. *La Iglesia y la producción agrícola en Puebla 1540-1795.* Mexico City: El Colegio de México, 1983.

Mendoza Briones, María Ofelia y Martha Terán. "Repercusiones de la política borbónica." Vol. II of *Historia general de Michoacán.* Mexico City: Instituto Michoacano de Cultura, 1989.

Molina Solís, Juan Francisco. *Historia del descubrimiento y conquista de Yucatán.* Mexico City: Ediciones Mensaje, 1943.

Morfi, Juan Agustín de. *Diario y derrotero (1777-1781).* ed. Eugenio del Hoyo and Malcolm D. McLean. Monterrey: Talleres de Impresiones, 1967.

Mota y Escobar, Alonso de la. *Descripción geográfica de los reynos de Nueva Galicia, Nueva Vizcaya y Nuevo León.* Guadalajara: Instituto Jaliscience de Antropología e Historia, 1966.

Motolinia, Toribio de. *Historia de los indios de la Nueva España.* Mexico City: Editorial Porrúa, 1969.

Muriel, Josefina. *Conventos de monjas en la Nueva España.* Mexico City: Editorial Santiago, 1946.

Novo, Salvador. "Recuerdos del Hotel Iturbide." *El palacio de Iturbide.* Mexico City: Fomento Cultural Banamex, 1972.

Nueva noticia del país que los españoles encontraron en el año de 1521 llamada Yucatán. Facsimile edition of a work published between 1521 and 1523. Mexico City: Universidad Nacional Autónoma de México / IEE / Imprenta Universitaria, 1940.

Olvera Calvo, María del Carmen and Ana Eugenia Reyes y Cabañas. "La importancia de las fuentes documentales para el estudio de los artistas y artesanos de la ciudad de México, Siglos XVI al XIX." Thesis. Facultad de Filosofía y Letras, Universidad Nacional Autónoma de México, 1991.

Orozco y Berra, Manuel. *Memoria para el plano de la ciudad de México, formada por orden del Ministerio de Fomento.* Mexico City: Imprenta Santiago White, 1867.

Ortega y Pérez Gallardo, Ricardo. *Historia genealógica de las familias más antiguas de México.* 3d ed. 3 vols. Mexico City: A. Carranza, 1908-1910.

Ortiz Macedo, Luis. *Los palacios nobiliarios de la Nuevas España.* Mexico City: Operadora de Bolsa, 1992.

Parra, Rafael de la. *San Diego de los Corrales, cinco siglos de historia.* [published by the author], 1977.

Pastor, Rodolfo and María de los Ángeles Romero Frizzi. "Expansión económica e integración cultural." Vol II of *Historia general de Michoacán.* Mexico City: Instituto Michoacano de Cultura, 1989, pp. 162-191.

Planat, P., ed. *Le Style Louis XVI; Recueil de Motifs Choisis d'Architecture Au XVIIIe Siecle. Palais, Chateaux, Monuments Publics, Hôtels Particulieres, Maisons, Églises . . . .* Paris: Librairie de la Construction Moderne, undated.

Porras Muñoz, Guillermo. *Iglesia y estado en la Nueva Vizcaya.* Mexico City: Universidad Nacional Autónoma de México, 1980.

Ramírez Montes, Mina. "La parroquia de San Miguel de Allende." *Anales del Instituto de Investigaciones Estéticas* 55 (1986).

Ramírez Romero, Esperanza. *Morelia en el espacio y en el tiempo. Defensa del patrimonio histórico y arquitectónico de la ciudad.* Mexico City: Gobierno del Estado de Michoacán, 1985.

Ripa, Cesare. *Iconología.* 2 vols. Madrid: Akal, 1987.

Rivera Cambas, Manuel. *México pintoresco, artístico y monumental.* 3 vols. Mexico City: Imprenta de la Reforma, 1882.

Romero de Terreros, Manuel. "La casa colonial." *Anales del Museo Nacional de Antropología, Historia y Etnología.* 3ª época, vol. V. (1913), pp. 161-209.

______. *Bocetos de la vida social novohispana.* Mexico City: Editorial Porrúa, 1944.

______. *Una casa del siglo XVIII en México.* Mexico City: Universidad Nacional Autónoma de México, 1957.

Rubial, Antonio. *La plaza, el palacio y el convento.* Mexico City: Consejo Nacional para la Cultura y las Artes, 1998.

Rubio Mañé, José Ignacio. *Monografía de los Montejo,* Mérida: Liga de Acción Social, 1930.

______. *La Casa de Montejo en Mérida de Yucatán.* Mexico City: Imprenta Universitaria, 1941.

______. *Archivo de la historia de Yucatán, Campeche y Tabasco.* Mexico City: Imprenta Aldina Robledo y Rosell, 1942.

Rubio Villanueva, Félix. *Revista Yucatán.* Edición especial para la primera Feria Nacional de Turismo, del 8 al 18 de febrero (1990).

Salvucci, Richard J. "Aspectos de un conflicto empresarial: el obraje de Balthasar de Sauto y la historia social de San Miguel el Grande, 1756-1771." *Anuario de Estudios Americanos* XXXVI. (1979), pp. 405-443.

Sánchez de Tagle, Esteban. "Una familia, una región. Los de la Canal de San Miguel el Grande en el siglo XVIII." *Memorias del Tercer Simposio de Historia de las Mentalidades, Familia y Poder en Nueva España.* Mexico City: Instituto Nacional de Antropología e Historia, 1991. pp. 115-124.

Sánchez Navarro y Peón, Carlos. *Memorias de un viejo palacio. (La casa del Banco de México).* Mexico City: Banco Nacional de México, 1951.

Sánchez, Gerardo. "Desamortización y secularización en Michoacán durante la reforma liberal. 1856-1863." Vol. III of *Historia general de Michoacán.* Mexico City: Instituto Michoacano de Cultura, 1989.

Saravia, Atanasio G. Vol. I of *Apuntes para la historia de la Nueva Vizcaya.* Mexico City: Universidad Nacional Autónoma de México, 1978.

______. "Padrón de la ciudad de Durango." Vol. IV of *Apuntes para la historia de la Nueva Vizcaya.* Mexico City: Universidad Nacional Autónoma de México, 1982.

Selman, Otto. *Mitología clásica ilustrada.* Barcelona: Editorial Vergara, 1960.

Sicilia IV. Milán: Attraverso L'Italia, 1933.

Sigaut, Nelly. "Azucenas entre espinas. El traslado del Convento de las monjas de Santa Catalina de Siena en Valladolid en 1738." *El arte y la vida cotidiana.* Mexico City: Instituto de Investigaciones Estéticas, Universidad Nacional Autónoma de México, 1995. pp. 199-215.

______ and Oscar Mazín. "El Cabildo de la Catedral de Valladolid y la construcción de las torres y fachadas de su iglesia." *Arte y Coerción.* Mexico City: Instituto de Investigaciónes Estéticas, Universidad Nacional Autónoma de México, 1992. pp. 109-122.

Tamarón y Romeral, Pedro. *Demostración del vastísimo obispado de la Nueva Vizcaya.* ed. Vito Alessio Robles. Mexico City: Robredo, 1937.

Tavera Alfaro, Xavier. Vol I of *Morelia en la época de la República Restaurada.* Mexico City: Instituto Michoacano de Cultura / El Colegio de Michoacán, 1988.

Toussaint, Manuel. *Paseos coloniales.* 2d ed. Mexico City: Instituto de Investigaciones Estéticas, Universidad Nacional Autónoma de México, 1962.

Tovar de Teresa, Guillermo. *México barroco.* Mexico City: Secretaría de Obras Públicas, 1981.

______. *La ciudad de los palacios: crónica de un patrimonio perdido.* 2 vols. Mexico City: Vuelta, 1990.

Vallebueno, Miguel. *Haciendas de Durango.* Mexico City: Gobierno del Estado de Durango, 1997.

Vázquez, Guillermina. "Una aproximación a la iconografía de la fachada de la Casa de Montejo." *Estudios acerca del arte novohispano. Homenaje a Elisa Vargas Lugo.* Mexico City: Universidad Nacional Autónoma de México, 1983.

Velázquez, María del Carmen. "Los reglamentos" and "Los indios gentiles apóstatas enemigos." *Tres estudios sobre las Provincias Internas de Nueva España.* Mexico City: El Colegio de México, 1979.

Zepeda Patterson, Jorge. "Michoacán en la época de Lázaro Cárdenas." Vol. IV of *Historia general de Michoacán.* Mexico City: Instituto Michoacano de Cultura, 1989.

Primary Sources

Archivo General de la Nación. *Bienes Nacionales*. 1023, doc. 81.

Archivo General de la Nación. *Historia. Obras públicas, Reales Cédulas, Vínculos y mayorazgos*.

Archivo General de la Nación (Mexico City). *Ordenanzas*. vol. 2, f. 220.

Archivo General de la Nación. (México City). *Vínculos y Mayorazgos*. vol. 15.

Archivo de la Catedral de Durango. Libro LXXVII, f. 212v.

Archivo de la Catedral de Durango. Libro LXXVII, f. 339v.

Archivo de la Catedral de Durango. Libro LXXVII, ff. 197v and 414.

Archivo de la Catedral de Durango. Libro VII, ff. 13v-14.

Archivo de Notarías del Estado de Durango. "Memoria testamentaria." 15 de agosto de 1799.

Archivo de Notarías de Morelia. Escribano Nicolás Pérez, contrato de venta. 10 de marzo de 1862. ff. 32v-34.

Archivo de Notarías de Morelia. Escribano Ramón Huerta. Escritura núm. 137. 17 de octubre de 1896. ff. 219-232.

Archivo de Notarías de Morelia. Escribano Ramón Huerta. Escritura Pública núm. 137. 17 de octubre de 1896. ff. 220-220v.

Archivo Histórico de la Academia de San Carlos.

Archivo Histórico de la Ciudad de México. Actas de cabildo, Artesanos y arquitectos, Juntas de Ciudad, Policía en general.

Archivo Histórico del Gobierno del Estado de Durango. "Diligencias de cobranza contra el conde de Súchil de los derechos de media anata durante su interinato como gobernador." exp. 63, cajón 14.

Archivo Parroquial de San Juan del Río. Libro de casamientos de Pánuco 1743-1766.

Autos de pedimento de el licenciado don Francisco Pérez de Espinosa, viceprefecto de el Oratorio de San Felipe Neri de la Villa de San Miguel el Grande, sobre el cumplimiento de una Real Cédula. 1738. Archivo General de la Nación (Mexico City). *Historia*. vol. 113, exp. 2-3, ff. 101-201.

Comprobante 2002, del Notario Público licenciado Javier Ibarrola, cited in Registro Público de la Propiedad del Estado de Michoacán. tomo 705, registro núm. 130749.

"Cuentas de cargo y data que Don Benito López, Administrador de los Diezmos de esta ciudad y sus anexos, presenta al Tribunal de Hacienda por los productos del año de 1798 y existencias de los que presentó del anterior de 97." Archivo Histórico Manuel Castañeda Ramírez, Fondo Cabildo, Sección Administración Pecuniaria, Serie Colecturía, Subserie Diezmos. f. 27v.

"Memorial ajustado de los autos que sigue don Agustín Durán, con la casa mortuoria del señor conde de San Mateo Valparaíso sobre paga de salarios." f. 9. [Found in: González-Polo "Memorial relativo al 'Palacio de Iturbide'." p. 83.]

Personal archives of Guillermo Berlanga Fernández de Córdoba.

Registro Público de la Propiedad del Estado de Michoacán, tomo 155, registro núm. 29471 and Escritura Pública. núm. 971 del 15 de noviembre del mismo año.

Registro Público de la Propiedad del Estado de Michoacán. tomo 705, registro núm. 130749, f. 300.

"Relación general de los bienes inventariados por fallecimiento del señor D. Miguel de Berrio y Zaldívar, conde de San Mateo Valparaíso, primer marqués de Xaral de Berrio." From the personal archives of Guillermo Berlanga Fernández de Córdoba. ff. 122 y 162v. [Found in: González-Polo. "El arquitecto Francisco Antonio Guerrero y Torres." p. 17.]

Sección de manuscritos de la Biblioteca Nacional de México: Cedularios.

Credits

Editorial Coordination	Cándida Fernández de Calderón Alberto Sarmiento Donate
Consultant	Juana Gutiérrez Haces
Design	Rolf Krayer Ana Celia Fernández (cover and title pages of chapters)
Photography	Fernando Cordero with the exception of: Rafael Doniz pp. 22, 51, 60, 61 and 62. Arturo González de Alba pp. 19, 20, 24, 25, 29, 39, 41, 43, 45-47, 53 and 55. Eniac Martínez p. 35. Mark Mogilner pp. 2, 8, 9, 37, 151, 153, 159, 166, 169, 173, 186, 192, 207, 213, 218, 221, 223, 229, 240, 244, 250 and cover. Jorge Vértiz pp. 30 and 31. Michel Zabé pp. 58 and 64.
Coordination of Design and Photography	Eva Lucía Reyes
Translation	Jeffrey Seefeldt
Electronic Layout	Firma Corporativa
Pre-press / DuPont Proof	Firma Digital

Palace of the Count de San Mateo de Valparaíso. Mexico City.

Acknowledgments

Fomento Cultural Banamex, A.C., is grateful to the following individuals and institutions for their valuable collaboration in the realization of this work:

Centro INAH (Instituto Nacional de Antropología e Historia) / Puebla
El Sol de Puebla
Museo Franz Mayer
Museo de la Ciudad de México
Museo Nacional de Historia del Castillo de Chapultepec
Sanborns Hermanos
Secretaría de Cultura del Estado de Puebla
Secretaría de Educación del Estado de Querétaro
Universidad Autónoma de Puebla
Universidad Nacional Autónoma de México

Rigoberto Benítez Trujillo
Vera Da Costa de Autrey
Enrique Doger Guerrero
Margarita Loera Chávez
Eduardo Merlo Juárez
José Francisco Ortiz Pedraza
Pedro Ángel Palou García
Esteban Paulín González
Antonio Pérez de la Peña
Marco Antonio Ponce de León Aguilar
Héctor Rivero Borrell
Rodrigo Rivero Lake
Andrés Romo Moreno
Gabriel Siade Barquet
Conrado Tostado Gutiérrez
Juan Pablo Urquiza

Palace of the Count de San Mateo de Valparaíso. Mexico City.

Pages 254 and 255.
Palace of the Count de San Mateo de Valparaíso. Mexico City.

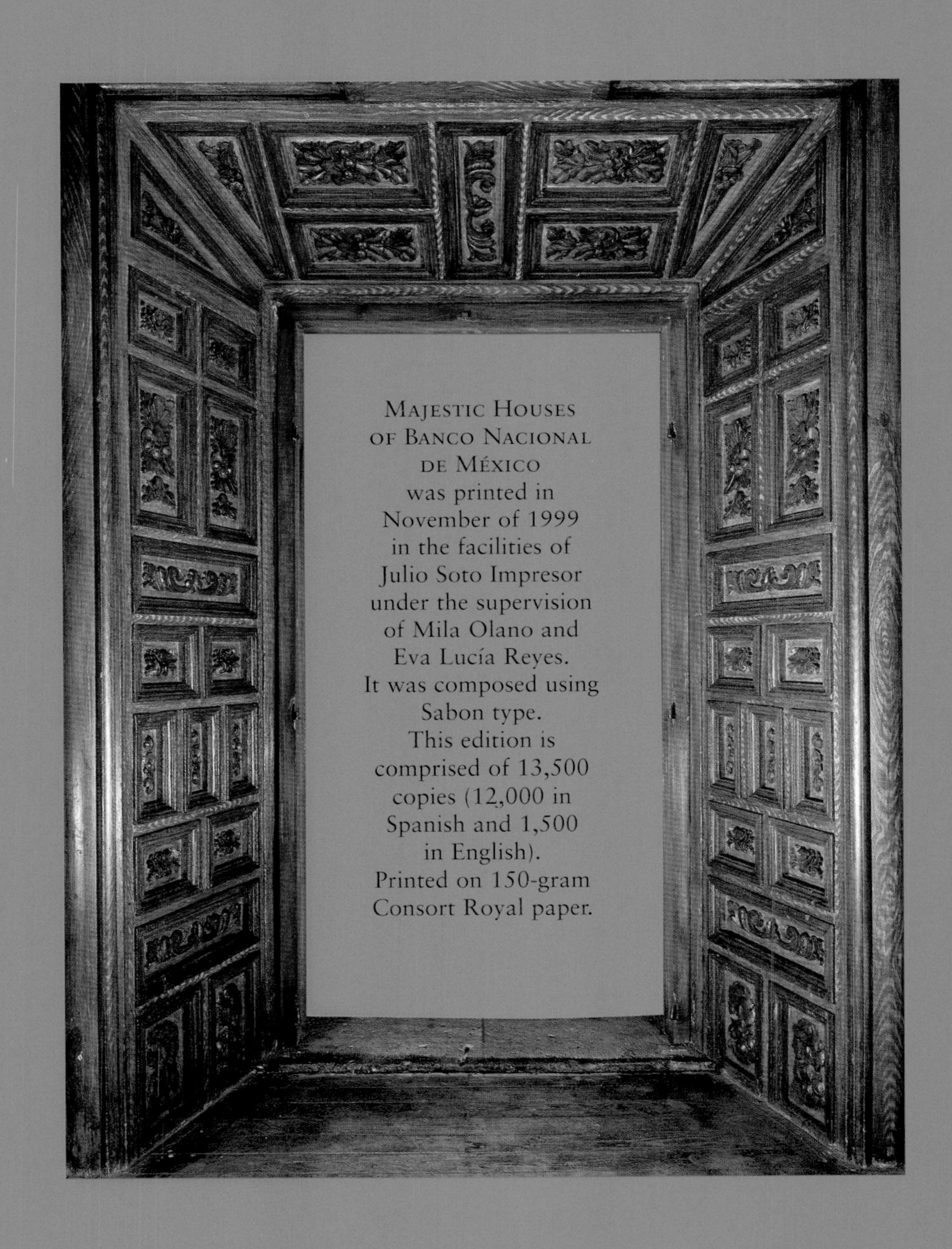

MAJESTIC HOUSES
OF BANCO NACIONAL
DE MÉXICO
was printed in
November of 1999
in the facilities of
Julio Soto Impresor
under the supervision
of Mila Olano and
Eva Lucía Reyes.
It was composed using
Sabon type.
This edition is
comprised of 13,500
copies (12,000 in
Spanish and 1,500
in English).
Printed on 150-gram
Consort Royal paper.